All My Heroes Have

FUR, FINS & FEATHERS

*An Animal Communicator's
Healing Journey of Awakening*

SHERRI A. LYNN

Open Door Publications

All My Heroes Have Fur, Fins & Feathers
An Animal Communicator's
Healing Journey of Awakening

The events told in this book are the author's memories of events. Some names have been changed to protect the privacy of the people involved.

Cover Design by Eric Labacz, labaczdesigns.com
Cover photograph by Greg Backman, gregbackman.com

Published by
Open Door Publications
Willow Spring, NC
OpenDoorPublications.com

Animals have brought more love, understanding, stability, and magic to my life than I could ever have imagined. They have led me, followed me, sat with me, and waited for me through the toughest and most challenging times of my life. Without them, I don't know where I would have ended up. When animals and I meet in our heart space, there is a perfection in life that makes time stand still. That experience, that feeling, still awes and inspires me. Animals are my heroes. This book is dedicated to every single one. With you, I feel safe, protected, and loved.

Contents

Prologue
All My Heroes
Have Fur, Fins, and Feathers

We all want the same things. We all want to feel safe, loved, protected, supported, validated, encouraged, trusted, special, heard, and so many other things. The seed of how we feel about ourselves starts very early. How we behave later in life also depends on that seed and how it is watered, fertilized, nurtured, and allowed to grow—or not. How true is the old saying: "You learn what you live with."

In the beginning you don't have a choice. You have your parents, grandparents, aunts, uncles, cousins, and siblings. If you're really lucky, all of them have their act together and can provide an environment that includes all those wonderful things and more. If you're somewhat lucky, most of them are equipped. Heck, you're still doing pretty well if only a few of them "get it." Even if you only have one semi-responsible older person in your life, you've hit the jackpot in my eyes.

I grew up in a loveless house feeling like an out of place piece of furniture most days. Sure, I received food, water, and shelter but not much in the way of teaching, encouragement, affection, kindness, attention, compassion, or nurturing. The only person who outwardly expressed genuine excitement to see me was my maternal granddad; sadly, he died when I was only 10 years old.

Mom's only sibling, a brother, died of polio in his teens. I often wondered if that was the cause of my maternal grandmother's lifelong bitterness and misery. Perhaps it also explained some of Mom's behavior: survivor's guilt? I don't remember Dad's parents; they both died when I was young. There were plenty of extended family around, but for the most part they were checked out as far as I was concerned. Since Dad was the second youngest, my aunts and uncles were all older and done with child-rearing. One aunt was the family matriarch, historian, and picture taker, but she was a homebody. Her time was spread thin with her own six children and, eventually, their children. Since I was the youngest cousin for some time, I was considered the nuisance cousin—the baby.

Functionally alcoholic parents, a bitter maternal grandmother, and a sociopathic narcissistic older sibling rounded out my "normal." There was a sense of balance with my parents, though. Dad was a likeable, easygoing guy with an awesome sense of humor who balanced Mom's unpredictable, uncontrollable rage. He had an incredible smile that could cancel out the evil behind the gritted teeth that passed for her smile—a look that served as a warning I was about to get another "lesson" from the wooden spoon. I was repeatedly hit so hard with that spoon my face would tingle. The unfounded beatings stemmed from lies told by my older sibling, lies told for the sheer pleasure that witnessing my beatings provided. Mom's unspoken motto was: "Hit first; clean the house and make dinner later." And my sibling knew it. Lying provided the pre-dinner entertainment. Once old enough to be my sitter, the entertainment morphed into physical torture and mental and emotional abuse. This was how it started. This was my "normal" childhood.

With the exception of three innocent youngsters, most people familiar with my abusers now fall into three categories: They are physically dead, dead to me, or so far in my rearview mirror any hope of a meaningful relationship with them is completely gone.

Dysfunction has regurgitating ripple effects. It also has incredible rewards. It took me over fifty years to summon the courage to speak up and walk away from the last of my abusers and the people who not only turned a blind eye, but made excuses for them.

It bears mentioning this book is not about everyone who failed me—the family and frenemies who figuratively left me bleeding by the side of the road. It is about my journey to self-discovery and the animals that *were* there for me. Each one gave selflessly; tirelessly. Many of them provided comfort and made me feel safe, loved, supported, and heard. Others taught me life lessons I could not possibly have received from anyone I share a bloodline with. This book celebrates and honors them. The amazing animals who make up my soul family—the furry, finned, and feathery critters who consistently provided the loving support my heart always knew was possible. They restored my faith and brought more magic to my life than I could have ever imagined. With heartfelt gratitude, this book is for them and the three youngsters I hope to eventually be reunited with.

Foreword

Arduous does not begin to adequately describe the task of contemplating this book's dedication. I wondered if I would even *have* a dedication page. I pondered mercilessly for weeks—even months. As I mentally paged through the thousands of people who have passed through my life, I struggled with who deserved such an honor. Certainly, there have been people worthy of this honor through *pieces* of my life; but who was truly there for *most* or *all* of it? As the book neared completion, it became crystal clear exactly who it was time for me to *see* and celebrate.

This special person has been by my side through all of it. She witnessed each and every single victory and defeat. Sometimes she led, sometimes she walked beside, sometimes she carried me, and sometimes she was tucked away deep in the darkness. Wherever she was and whatever role she played, she was patient, kind, and loving to others. She spoke, and she listened. She felt all the joys and all the sorrows described in this book. Her patience, tenacity, and imagination led the way to this magical adventure of working with and speaking to animals. Without her, none of this would have been possible.

With heartfelt gratitude, I honor my inner child. Her playfulness and love for all beings has guided me through life's harshest moments. Please help me honor her by embracing your own inner child and the special children in your life. Let's play!

Chapter 1
Tom, My First Orange Cat

"I can't. I just can't do it anymore," I cried to my girlfriend. "Look at him! He's trying to run away from me...he hates me now." Shaking, I continued. "What am I doing?" I slid down the cabinets I was leaning against to steady myself, then landed on the kitchen floor. I was now sobbing. I held my face in my hands as I tried repeatedly to swallow the burning emotional lump in my throat.

"This isn't fair to either of us anymore," I said. "It breaks my heart to watch him suffer without it, yet he tries his best to bolt when I grab the pill bottle. This torment every day is too much, for both of us."

Tom and I were both drooling now—me from the first raw and real emotion I'd ever been able to express safely with no one to deliberately mock me or tell me they'd give me something to cry about, and my big orange cat in anticipation of receiving his dreaded heart medication.

Tom was the last kitten left from a litter his calico mom, who had belonged to us, had delivered. We were able to find homes for all but him. He was my very first orange cat. I don't remember exactly how old I was when he was born, but I do remember the life events he saw me through. Those painful and traumatic childhood memories come back to me in fragments, not necessarily chronologically. Sometimes they bounce around. Sometimes pieces are missing.

Through the years I saw different therapists, but they only got me so far. They helped me recognize many of my adult behaviors were normal for someone who grew up like I had. They explained the difference between coping and true healing. They all tried with their one- or two-hour-a-week sessions—for years. I made a lot of progress, but in the end they ALL missed the biggest abuse of all. That one, the ugliest one, would be uncovered in my 50s. And there would be another special cat to see me through that one.

Healing from just one adverse childhood experience can be a lifelong process, imagine having several. Imagine thinking your experiences are normal. Even the best of therapists can only help uncover so much. Therapists pick the scab and leave you bleeding until the following appointment. Subject matter experts such as doctors and psychiatrists write books you can have access to at any time. John Bradshaw and Bessel van der Kolk have spent their careers trying to decipher how the injured brain recovers from trauma, abuse, and post-traumatic stress disorder (PTSD), especially that which occurred during the different phases of childhood development. Bradshaw and van der Kolk's books, *Homecoming: Reclaiming and Healing Your Inner Child* and *The Body Keeps the Score*, respectively, have helped me tremendously in my healing journey. The animals that have come and gone in my lifetime were there when the therapists weren't.

Tom led the way.

Tom was there as I struggled through my teens when I first came to understand the molestation I had endured by not one, but two men (female family members were with them) was not okay. He was there when I started drinking, taking pills, smoking weed, and doing other things to cope with difficult life situations. He was there the morning I found my mother dead from a heart attack. At 20 years old many people thought I would go crazy living in the house where I found her. There was no room in my dad's or grandmother's houses so I moved in with a friend and her mother for a while. Tom waited patiently for me for nearly two years, living outside at my dad's house, because Dad didn't allow animals in the house. I finally moved into Dad's unfinished basement until I could buy a home of my own. Eventually, after a good night of drinking, I snuck him into my area in the basement for comfort. His purring was just loud enough to distract me from the self-defeating thoughts that filled my head. He slept on my pillow that night and every night after, just like he had before we were suddenly uprooted from my mother's house after her death.

Looking back, I didn't learn much about pet care from either of my parents. We took our pets to the free rabies clinic for shots and to the vet when they were injured or sick. At that time neutering wasn't routinely done either. Tom was an indoor/outdoor cat. He would go out during the day and do "Tom" things, and then come home at night for dinner and to sleep on my pillow. Once when I was about 18 years old, he was gone for a few days. When he finally came home, his paw was huge—clearly swollen from an infection. I rushed him to the vet. In addition to lancing and draining the wound that had clearly been obtained during a cat fight, the vet also neutered him.

When my friend and I went to pick him up, I was told how much he had missed me. He wouldn't eat or drink a thing. He didn't even potty while he was there! When the technician carried him out (we didn't even have a proper carrier in those days), he stretched out his legs in my direction and let out the loudest Tom Cat meow I had ever heard. My boy wanted me! He sat quietly on my lap for the six-mile or so ride home. When we were about four blocks from the house, I felt an incredibly warm sensation in my lap that slowly crept down and around my thighs, followed immediately by the stench of two-day old, stale, antibiotic-filled tomcat urine. I quickly brought Tom inside and returned to clean the lake of urine on the seat of my friend's car. Despite our best attempts to absorb the liquid and wipe down the seat, we were not successful in completely removing the odor. The car was left with the scent of damp Pine-Sol with a hint of stale urine. When time didn't get rid of the odor, my friend got rid of the car.

Not too long afterwards Tom was gone again for a bit of a stretch. This time, I was really worried and canvassed the neighborhood—no Tom. I called the shelter to see if they picked up any orange cats and was met with, "Yeah, we have orange cats. Come take a look." I drove there to find my boy in kitty cat jail. When he saw me he let out the same gut-wrenching meow as he had the day I picked him up from the vet. As I paid his bail, the shelter worker told me how dumb my cat was. Tom walked right into a trap set for another cat, and they hadn't even put any food in it yet! Tom wasn't dumb; he was a cat and curious and loving and so much more. Stupid shelter worker. I was about 18 or 19 years old at the time.

After sneaking him into Dad's basement for over a year, I finally managed to save enough money to buy my own home. I didn't move Tom in right away because it was a handyman special and required some work. A few weeks in, a well-meaning friend showed up with a gray kitten as a housewarming present. I had mixed feelings about the kitten moving in before Tom, but I accepted him. It wasn't long afterwards I fetched Tom; after all, he had to show the new kitten the ropes. Tom and Mission were inseparable. I had forgotten what it was like to have a kitten, and Tom did his best to keep him out of trouble.

Tom taught Mission when it's night-night time: A cat's place is at their master's head purring them to sleep. That's when I discovered two cats are better than one! Over time, I learned about proper cat care, including dental work, regular exams, and keeping them indoors. During one exam I was told my aging cat's heart was compromised, and medicine would help. It broke my heart to see Tom slowing down. After all, he had showered me with more unconditional love, care, patience, and concern than anyone else in my life. The process of giving Tom his meds was okay at first— until he realized it was going to be every day. My easygoing, calm, cool cat now ran away from me when the meds came out. When I finally caught him, he looked up at me with sadness in his eyes that tore at my heart. He would start to drool in preparation for the pill. The daily struggle we endured getting his meds in was not fair to either of us. He was failing. My boy had been my faithful companion for 18 years. That's a really good run for a cat, especially one that spent a good portion of his time outdoors doing tomcat things.

On a snowy winter day, I said goodbye to Tom in my kitchen. I couldn't bear to take him to the vet to have it done. What I didn't realize at the time was that the incomplete grieving of my grandfather's death when I was nine years old and my mother's sudden death when I was 20 years old was causing incredibly painful flashbacks and PTSD. In those moments I was simultaneously in pain and numb. My girlfriend and a family member took Tom to the vet for me while my now several years sober Dad struggled for hours to dig a hole in the solid winter ground, and I stayed home and cried. I cried for days. I'm crying now, more than 25 years later, as I write about it. To this day, I regret my decision. I should have been at the vet with Tom when he took his last breath—the way he was there for me through so many painful life-altering moments. *Mine* should have been the last face he saw as he transitioned, not the face of the first (and worst) of my abusers. If I could take back any moment in time, it would be that one. He deserved better. I know that now, but I didn't know it then.

Dear Tom, thank you for that painful lesson. There have been many cats since you. I have never made that mistake again. Rest in peace, my sweet boy.

Chapter 2
Turbo

Kittens! Who doesn't love kittens? They are warm and fuzzy, soft and cuddly. Their rhythmic purring calms and soothes the soul. Simply being in their presence brings out the best in people. Right? It has taken me half a lifetime to realize that. Sadly, my older sibling is not "most people."

"Tennnnn, ninnnnne, eiiiiight," a voice said excitedly as a kitten was held out in front between both hands with straightened arms. "Sevennnnn, sixxxxxx, fiiiiive,"—the person's arms rose and the kitten lifted—"fourrrrrr, threeeeeee, twooooo,"—the kitten was lifted higher and higher, almost overhead now—"onnnnnne, blastoff!" The limp kitten was sharply turned upside down with its head now headed straight for the grass. It was stopped abruptly just short of the grass—just short of crashing headfirst. Laughter followed. Being seven years younger, I laughed then, too. I was maybe three or four years old and didn't know any better.

"You try now."

I was encouraged to imitate—and did—with a different kitten from the pile as the mother cat watched. It was called rocket ship. That scene and my participation as an obedient sibling still make me sick more than five decades later. Many years later, as an adult with a loving nature and conscience, I have subliminally worked to make amends for being taught what "was fun" for kittens.

Enter Turbo.

"Never again," I uttered into the phone. "I just lost Tom and vowed I wouldn't do it again. Once Mission goes, that's it. The pain of losing them is just too much."

The voice at the other end of the phone replied, "But he's just a kitten. Her boyfriend wants him gone by the end of the day or he's going to the shelter. You know what happens then. They're already overcrowded."

"Grrrr, I really don't want to. It's too soon. What color is it?" I asked.

"Orange. He's the cutest little orange kitten" was the response.

"Oh my God," I said. "Okay, but I'm taking him under protest."

It was an early morning weekend call, and I wasn't thinking clearly. I was somewhere between still drunk, hungover, and dehydrated. Always the people pleaser, I never learned how to set proper boundaries as a youngster so my "no's" were weak at best. I couldn't disappoint—no matter what was asked of me—and most people knew it. Mission had lost his older brother, and now he was going to be one to an orange kitten found crying outside someone's bedroom window.

My pets usually name themselves immediately or within a few days. This new kitten was no exception. He was incredibly nimble, athletic, and unbelievably fast for his age and size. "Turbo," I said. As soon as I said it out loud, he turned to look at me. "His name is undeniably Turbo!" It was decided.

Turbo was a bit of an odd kitten. He didn't follow Mission around to learn the ropes, like younger siblings do. Instead, he figured things out his own way. He was strong enough to be his own cat, even as a kitten. Turbo was bold and fiercely independent. If he wanted something, he was going to go for it—regardless of the consequences.

I left an opened pint of half-and-half on the kitchen counter. Turbo wanted it. In a flash he was on the counter, grabbed the pint in his mouth, and landed back on the floor. The container remained upright the whole time. I swear his feet didn't even touch the counter; his body just twisted to change directions in midair. I stopped him just before he tipped the carton to get to the contents. He was so close—but no milk.

Another day I had just baked a tray of wings of fire. They are similar to Buffalo wings, only hotter. The hot cookie sheet was on the counter with the spicy hot wings. Here came Turbo. He catapulted himself through the air like one of the Flying Wallendas. He latched his jaws onto a hot fire wing like it was a trapeze bar. Just like he did with the half-and-half container, he changed directions while airborne and landed on the kitchen floor with the wing still in his mouth. It didn't take long for him to realize the wings were way too hot for him. On days like those he was called Bad Ass.

Turbo and Mission didn't fight, but they also didn't play together. I wondered if it was the age difference or something else. A friend had a cat about the same age as Turbo so we decided to try a playdate. Punk came over, and the two seemed to get along well while Mission watched. We decided to do a sleepover. I brought Turbo to Punk's house after dinner one night and hung around just long enough to make sure they were okay. My friend showed Turbo where the litter box and water were, and I left. Not much after sunrise I got a call. "Come get your cat!"

"Uh oh, what happened?" I asked.

"I woke up to the sound of scratching and the smell of fresh cat shit" was the reply. "Freaking cat shit next to the bed, and Turbo was trying to bury it with my sweatshirt!" she continued.

I retrieved Bad Ass and brought him home. Funny for me, not so funny for my friend and the shitty situation she was put in.

As Turbo matured, it became clear he wasn't like my other cats. He had a wild side. Now I know he was probably feral. Despite being handled a lot as a kitten, he was not happy inside. Not happy at all. He destroyed curtains and furniture legs. Door trim he would climb like trees or use to sharpen his claws. It was fascinating to watch but expensive to fix. When the screen door was exposed, he would leap onto the top section and hold onto it like Spiderman. To reinforce the screen, I eventually put chicken wire on it. I didn't dare open the door or he would bolt. Occasionally, "helpful" friends would let him out despite my insistence not to. Turbo's route was always the same. He would race out of the house, down the driveway, across the street, and up into the neighbor's tree.

Since I couldn't fight Turbo's deep desire to be outside, I tried working with it. I bought a harness and a leash. *I'll take it slow*, I thought. Get him used to the harness, attach the leash, and try walking him inside, and then outside. He clearly didn't like having anything on his body. He shook and rolled and rubbed trying to get the harness off. I started with just a few minutes at a time and increased the duration gradually. In the days that followed, he was comfortable enough for me to attach the leash. We stood there. I gave a gentle tug, and he threw himself to the ground. I picked him back up to his feet and tried again. Plop. I begged. I pleaded. I tried reasoning. I felt horrible.

"Come on, buddy. I'm doing this so you can spend time outside—safely" I pleaded. "There's no other way. You have to meet me halfway."

He finally took a few steps on the leash, and we went outside.

Outside on the leash, Turbo threw himself onto the grass and rolled around. It was hard to say whether he was happy or not. I stayed outside with him for a while before calling it quits and bringing him back inside for the night. I would keep trying.

One day I hooked his leash to the clothesline for a little more freedom. Since Turbo seemed content to lie on the driveway and soak up the sun, I left him outside while I went inside for a drink. Moments later, I returned to an empty harness. Glancing across the street, I saw Turbo high in his favorite tree. On days like these, he was called Houdini. Each time he escaped I knew exactly where to find him—every time but once.

It was a Saturday morning, nine-thirty, ten o'clock at best. The cats were fed and watered, and their litter boxes were cleaned. After a quick look around I deemed it was safe to take the trash out—or so I thought. Always the opportunist, the door only had to be partially unlatched for Turbo to nose his way through and out. And he did. As soon as I got outside to chase him, I heard a car coming down the street. My heart started to race as I watched in horror as Turbo ran in the direction of his favorite tree—on the other side of the street. I could hear the car approaching the end of my driveway just as Turbo was.

The only thing I could do was yell his name in the hope he would stop, stop short of the street—and the car. I screamed. "TURBO!"

He turned to look just as his body went under and up over the car's front tire. The thump his body made when it hit the top of the wheel well is still fresh in my mind. I ran to him and scooped him up in my arms. He was seizing and convulsing and bleeding as I held him. I yelled at the driver. I yelled for someone to call a vet, the police—somebody, anybody. I could feel his warm blood leaving his body, rhythmically with each heartbeat—there was so much of it. It was everywhere. On my arms, my shirt, my thighs, the road. I cradled him like a baby as his eyes rolled back in his head. His heart and seizing stopped before the police officer even rolled up. I just held him—and cried. On this day he was called Free.

Chapter 3
Rewriting History With Goldie

The brain is a funny thing. Not "ha ha" funny but tricky funny. It can take a really good present-day experience and jolt you back in time to a lousy memory. I think I'm past my past, and then it comes back up—like a bad meal. There is good news in all of this, though. The more I persevere, the faster I catch myself repeating old and destructive patterns and the faster I can change course. Over the last few years I have brought more loving, supportive people (and animals) into my life. I am grateful to be creating better memories every chance I get.

At one of the docks at Raystown Lake in Pennsylvania, there is a spot where you can hand-feed dog kibble to giant goldfish, otherwise known as carp. Being a lover of ALL critters, I had to try it. When the fish saw me approaching with food in my hand, hundreds rushed over, creating an indescribable bubbling surge of water. Just like at the start of a competitive open water swim, the fish were all fighting for the best position. I squealed with delight like a little kid. I looked over at my new girlfriend who was beaming at my childlike excitement. It felt good to have someone genuinely happy to see me having a good time.

Enter flashback.

I didn't want the money. I never wanted the money—the guilt money. I came to understand it was guilt money from my divorced father on his weekly Thursday visitation day. It was money given to me as a substitute for his time and attention. Money to keep me busy while he found something else to do such as take a nap or drink beer on the porch with the neighborhood men who lived next door to Dad's house.

This week was special, though. The carnival was in town. Back then we rode seatbelt free. We rode with the windows rolled down in his Salem cigarette smoke-filled blue Bonneville to the other end of town. I couldn't contain my excitement at actually going someplace with Dad! We were really going to *do* something together! This was a big day indeed!

I could smell the popcorn and cotton candy. I saw loads and loads of people milling around games and rides and the food and ticket booths. There were so many sounds and lights and smells. The place was just bustling with activity. I was here. With my Dad!

He handed me money and told me to go play the games; he'd catch up. Confused, I said, "Huh?"

"Go ahead, I'll find you."

Hesitantly, I walked away. I wasn't one to play the "wheels." I preferred the games of skill. I'd try to knock over the fuzzy, stuffed cats or milk jugs with a baseball or toss a dime on a plate or in an ashtray or juice glass. When the money ran out, I found Dad—next to the beer truck. He wasn't interested in the ashtrays, plates, or glasses I had won. He asked if I was having a good time and, without actually listening for an answer, he lit another cigarette, dished out more money, and waved me away.

This time I hit it big! I tossed a ping-pong ball into a small goldfish bowl. The bowl wasn't much bigger than a softball. Holy crap! I won a fish! I looked around to see if Dad saw it—to see if he HAD "caught up" so he could celebrate with me, be excited for me, be proud of me. No Dad. He was still by the beer truck. I was ready to go home to my mother with my new fish, Goldie.

"You won whaaaaat?" my mother asked as I hurried into the house.

"A fish. A goldfish," I replied as I excitedly held out the baggie with the fish in it. She mumbled something under her breath that I couldn't hear. It probably wasn't something an eight-year-old should have heard anyway. Clearly annoyed that we now had "another mouth to feed" because, you know, goldfish eat so much, she snapped, "If it survives the night in that baggie, we'll have to get a proper fish bowl, food, and supplies." I think secretly she hoped it wouldn't make it. In the morning Goldie was still alive. I celebrated—alone.

My mother dutifully took me to the store to get what we needed to properly care for Goldie. I don't know who she was madder at: me, Dad, Goldie, or herself. I remember thinking it should have been a happy time, like it was over 45 years later at Raystown Lake.

In hindsight, Goldie mirrored my childhood. Stay small, out of the way, don't ask for much, and just keep chasing your tail in circles. As far as fish go, Goldie was around a long time. I remember Goldie's long, flowing tail grew nearly as long as its body. I also remember catching Mom talking to Goldie—in a nice way. Maybe that's what Goldie's purpose was: to soften her ever so slightly.

I see light at the end of the tunnel. My painful flashbacks are also subsiding. Rewriting history takes time. I choose to think of the experience at Raystown Lake as Goldie and her ancestors gathering to celebrate how far I've come in my healing journey. Tossing a piece of kibble into the waiting mouth of a carp was just like tossing a ping-pong ball into a waiting fishbowl. It's a good memory now. Thank you, Goldie, and the loving, supportive people by my side today—you know who you are.

Chapter 4
Divine Intervention

"STOP THE CAR! STOP THE CAR!" I yelled as I beat on the dashboard with my hands and stomped my feet on the floorboard.

My friend had not yet spotted what I had. Lying motionless on the side of the road was a medium-sized bundle of fur with legs that had just gotten hit by a car.

"The dog, the dog!" I pointed and shouted as I left the car and shot across the highway without even looking. It was weird. I went from calmly sitting in a car to kneeling beside a motionless body in a blink—as if transported there by a superior being.

The dog was in sorry shape. His back leg was twisted into an S-shape, his eyes were rolled back into his head, blood was oozing out of his nose, and mucous was draining from his mouth. I was divinely guided to put my hands on this mangled mess of a dog. In my head and heart, I said to myself, *If it's going to happen, please let it happen quickly. Please don't let this little guy suffer.*

There was chaos all around.

"I called the police, they're on their way," one woman said.

Another said, "I can't believe the guy just kept going. Who does that?"

The woman who owned the dog was on the other side of the highway holding her face in both hands like the kid in the movie *Home Alone.* "I have little kids," she cried. "They can't see this."

"Sweetie, you need to move off to the side of the road before you get hit, too," another lady nudged me.

I took notice of the chaos around me and realized how incredibly safe, calm, and connected I felt. I remember a brief moment when I felt like laughing at the lady who told me to move off the road. *Do you even know who I am?* was the thought that floated through my brain. It was in that moment I realized I was not the only occupant in my body. Something divine was working through me. I felt safer and more protected than I ever had in my life so I just went with it.

The dog started seizing. His frail body was now twitching and contorting uncontrollably. He lost his bowels. The stench of hot, steamy dog poop wafting in the air didn't rattle me at all. I continued to hold my position. My friend ran to her car and returned with a sweatshirt. With my hands still on the dog, she lovingly placed her sweatshirt on his body. The seizing stopped. He looked at peace. I continued to allow this divine energy to flow through me into his apparently lifeless body.

Several minutes had passed. I finally lifted his little head with one hand and asked, "Little guy, what's going on? Are you still in there?"

In a flash he scrambled to his feet and made an attempt to dart back across the highway. Quickly, I wrapped my arms around his body and tackled him.

"Dude, the first time didn't work out so well. You're not doing it again—not on my watch," I muttered to him.

I heard a car door slam and yelling from behind. It was the dog's human daddy, annoyed and yelling at his wife. I don't remember what all he said but could tell from his tone he was not happy. He came, scooped up the now wriggling-to-get-free dog, and headed for his backyard, mumbling under his breath. I asked if I could follow and wash my arms at their house. He said something that resembled an "okay."

In the couple's kitchen I told the man's wife what I knew. Leg S-shaped, seizure, blood, mucous, eyes rolled back in his head. I said he needs to go to the vet.

With that, the husband entered and said, "I'm not so sure about that."

My initial thought was *Oh no! The dog must have dropped dead from internal injuries.* Instead, I asked him, "What do you mean?"

He replied happily, "The dog is putting weight on his leg. Come look."

In the time it took me to dry my arms with a paper towel and follow the man outside, sure enough, the dog was running around in the backyard as if nothing happened. I was dumbfounded. I looked at the man and said, "Dude, I can't even believe this. I'd swear your dog was going to die in my arms."

I left the family my contact information as I numbly took my leave. It was then that I noticed my hands. They were tingling and pulsing like I'd never felt before. They still pulse like that every time I tell what happened that day. The policeman arrived, and I passed by the dog on the lawn as I shuffled toward the car. My friend was waiting patiently to console me.

"I'm sorry," she said.

"For what?" I said.

"You did all you could," she continued.

"The dog is fine," I said. In disbelief I pointed in the direction of the dog. "See?"

"Oh, I just thought they had another dog," she said.

Tears began to flow as the raw emotion of what happened rose up from deep inside me. I pointed and said, "That's the dog! I just, I just witnessed a miracle."

By all accounts this dog was destined to cross the rainbow bridge that day. Instead, an earth angel guided by divine intervention made sure he was safely returned to his family and the little kids who loved him. The family called the next day to tell me the vet said, "He's fine. He's just going to be sore for a few days." I also learned the irony that he was named after a football player on the Giants. I hope that pup knows the wonderful gift of healing he revealed to me that day. On behalf of all the animals that have followed, a heartfelt thanks to this one for opening the door. I remain humbled and awestruck by this powerful gift and perfect timing.

This incredible incident started my journey to awakening.

Chapter 5
Sunshine

They find you. They just do. "They" are those extremely special animals meant for you and no one else. Sometimes they do it alone, and sometimes they conspire with other animals or people to get to you. They are so much smarter than you could ever hope to be. Sunshine was that cat.

"Free to good home: kittens," the ad read.

It was the day after Turbo's traumatic exit from this lifetime. I kept having flashbacks of yesterday's scene—the blood, the convulsing, the pain and agony. Despite not being particularly close, Mission was pacing from room to room, obviously looking for his younger brother. The yowling that accompanied the pacing was deep, long, frequent, and loud—soulful. It brought me to tears. Still distraught myself, I didn't have the emotional bandwidth to comfort Mission. There was nothing I could do. He was mourning in a way I had never experienced. It was soul-crushing, to say the least. To complicate matters, my heart and gut weren't exactly working together yet. I felt lost. During a very brief silence, a voice in my head whispered, "Don't think too far ahead. Just do the next right thing." I read the ad again and called. The free kittens were in the next town.

"When can we come see them?" I asked.

"You can come now if you want" was the answer. Off we went!

The mamma cat and her kittens were in a box on the porch. Some were squirming, some were nursing, and some were sleeping. They were adorable, as all kittens are. It didn't take long for me and my girlfriend to settle on a tiny orange female. Holding her for the first time warmed my heart as the morning sun simultaneously warmed my face. The connection was made, and her name was clear.

"Her name is Sunshine. Welcome to my life, Sunshine. Let's take you home to meet your brother, Mission."

It wasn't long before I realized the newspaper ad should have read: "fleas to a good home." Sunshine was riddled with fleas! And she shared them with Mission. The two cats spread the fleas throughout the house.

"At least you two are working together," I mumbled to them.

Cats love car rides about as much as they love baths so when the flea baths didn't work, a car ride was in order while the flea bombs did their job. Once wasn't enough; the process had to be repeated a few times. Thankfully, things got better.

Sunshine was smart, loving, sweet, and cuddly. She was also at least as athletic as Turbo and loved to play—inside! She loved playing cat in the middle. We would lob toys over her head, and she would leap as high as a pole vaulter to nab them. Neither she nor Mission had any desire to go outside—ever. They were happy to watch the birds and squirrels from their window perches.

While Mission was content to nap and entertain himself during the day, Sunshine was always nearby. She loved attention and loved being the center of attention. If I came home from work crabby, Sunshine would get my attention, walk me into the living room, and sit by the stereo. It was her way of telling me to turn on the music and dance with her. I would pick her up and hold her one paw as if we were ballroom dancing. We would twirl and dip—she loved it probably more than I did!

Sunshine also included me in her daily grooming. She licked my fingers and tilted her head so I could brush the side of her face with my freshly licked fingers. She would lick several times; I would brush the side of her face two or three times, and then she would lick again. We did this a few times for each side of her face. She always found ways to shift me out of a lousy mood *and* get what she wanted in the process. I learned so much about loving, attention, and asking for what you need from her.

Sunshine was around when I first discovered my special gift and sought training to learn how to do Reiki. She insisted I practice on her daily. She would not allow me to sleep on my left side. Each night I would lie on my right side, spooning her with my left hand, delivering Reiki to her tiny body. If and when I rolled over to my left side, she would wake up and start gently picking at my pajamas until I rolled back over "into position." This picking at my pajamas happened nearly every single night.

Things in the household were awesome until a beautiful Maine Coon kitty showed up in the yard. Someone tossed her out like a piece of trash. She was living on the streets like a bum. As a result, her name became Skidrow. Once I took her to the vet, she moved into the house with Sunshine and Mission. Mission could care less, but Sunshine was not happy. My loving, docile, orange cat did not welcome this interloper with open paws. Sunshine growled, hissed, and executed rapid-fire rap-tap-tap assaults on poor Skidrow's head whenever she got too close. It took months before all three cats could sleep on the bed peacefully at night. Sometimes Sunshine was so angry she'd sleep in another room. On those nights I would spoon Skidrow.

At the age of ten years, Sunshine was diagnosed with a heart murmur, and shortly afterwards hyperthyroidism was added to her medical chart. Her medicine for hyperthyroidism would eventually affect her kidneys, and she would need prescription cat food. I had a terrible time accepting the news, but my Sunshine kept her whiskers up and took it all in stride. I had the notion she would be the first of the three to "go," and it saddened me. She was so special and connected to me I couldn't bear the thought. As it turned out, Mission got cancer and needed help crossing over; years later, Skidrow died suddenly from an undetected heart condition. The girlfriend who helped pick Sunshine and I also parted ways. It was just the two of us—me and Sunshine—for a while.

I felt bad for Sunshine being home alone while I was at work or out with friends so I consulted an animal communicator. The communicator explained since Sunshine was in her golden years, she really didn't want to deal with a young kitten. She further explained Sunshine knew how hard it was going to be for me when she passed if there were no other cats in the house. Sunshine stated she would be okay with a cat that was a few years old.

Enter Boo.

It was 2012. A large, buff-colored cat started showing up outside during mealtime. He was dirty and angry, and had scratches and patches of missing fur that were clearly battle wounds from his life on the street. His head hung low, and his eyes were cast downward. I left food and water out whenever I saw him. He started coming to the house regularly. Eventually, I got him neutered, and he made his way into the house.

His whole story is another chapter, but he is introduced here because his life overlapped and intertwined with Sunshine's life.

When Boo first entered the house, it was a disaster! Both cats went on hunger strikes as they expressed their displeasure with their new living arrangements. Sunshine somehow knew Boo was just an overgrown kitten, and Boo thought he would still be able to go outside. Eventually, Boo gave in and ate, but Sunshine had to be taken to the vet for fluids and an appetite stimulant for her to start eating again.

Over time Boo and Sunshine became pals. Initially, unbeknown to me, Sunshine even explained to Boo how to behave after she was gone. I loved how much more life Boo's presence brought to Sunshine. They played tag at least once a day. Boo was always the chaser, and Sunshine was always the chasee. Sunshine smiled while being chased by her younger brother, and Boo jogged contently behind as he tried not to outrun her. Remembering the sound of the chase through the house still makes me smile.

One night Sunshine gave me a big scare. I came home to find her dragging herself across the kitchen floor to greet me. Her back half was completely useless; even her toes were cold. I immediately started giving her Reiki. A trip to the emergency vet resulted in a few options for what it could be and how to handle it. Euthanasia was one of those options. It was the first option off the table. I brought her home with medications and a "Good luck. We're here all night" from the veterinarian.

I made her comfortable and continued to send her Reiki. I asked for divine guidance and support. I laid a towel in the bed next to me in Sunshine's "spot" in case she had a potty accident, and we went to sleep. Hours later, she fidgeted so I held her backside up as she used the litterbox. We went about our days as normally as we could. I continued to assist her in the litterbox and helped her gain access to her favorite nap spots.

Despite needing assistance in the litterbox, she remained continent through the whole ordeal and improved daily. I later came to understand that she had had an aortic blood clot, and that

most cats are euthanized within 48 hours of having one. Not my resilient girl! Within weeks she resumed her daily game of tag and regained nearly all of her mobility. The only area that didn't come back was the last section of her foot. It tended to drag a little bit but did not impede the quality of life she enjoyed.

Two years after recovering from the blood clot, I noticed Sunshine was slowing down. Her breathing was uneasy, and her appetite was not as hearty. She was winded after playing tag and had to rest more often. She played tag daily up until four days before she needed assistance leaving her tired body.

One morning she collapsed in the litterbox, and I knew it was time. At 19 years old, my beautiful, pretty, funny, loving, resilient, sunshiny, little girl had lived more than the nine lives most cats are given. I held her and kissed her and rubbed my face on her fur and petted her as we drove to the vet's office. She was smiling. She had lived a good life. I held back tears and was brave for her. She had given me so much in those 19 years. She taught me love, patience, resilience, playfulness, tenacity, forgiveness, courage, and so much more.

She was content. The port was in, the sedative administered.

"Let me know when you're ready," the veterinarian said.

"She's been a part of my life for so long, I honestly don't know if I'll ever be ready," I replied.

With that, my sweet Sunshine stretched out her paw with the port in it as if to say "I've lived a good life. It's time. I'm ready."

We all looked at each other in disbelief. Sunshine knew exactly what she was doing. It was her final act of love for me. She did not want me to second-guess or regret my decision.

With a burning lump in my throat and tears in my eyes, I managed to choke out the words, "It's time, and she's made her wishes clear. Goodbye, sweet girl, and thank you."

Sunshine was wrapped in her favorite blanket and lovingly placed in her favorite bed. She was buried beside the others who had gone before her. The flea-to-good-home kitty who chose to spend 19 good years with me had been returned to the soil from which she came.

I long for the day when we meet again. Your love and lessons will forever be in my heart. Thank you for providing me the love and support I always knew existed. I promise to follow your example with how I live and treat others.

Chapter 6
Boo Boo Kitty

He was big, bad, battered, and angry. He was buff in both color and stature. The dirty, nasty-looking cat with scratches and patches of missing fur that showed up in my yard one day. He stared at me from the end of the driveway. With shoulders hunched like a vulture over roadkill, he stood, glared at me, and demanded food. I obliged. He ate and disappeared.

Over time he came more regularly and stayed longer. He stood taller and made more eye contact. The scratches turned to scabs, and the missing fur started to grow back. I referred to him as "Boo Boo Kitty" because of his obvious battle scars. I was disappointed and worried on the days he didn't show up, wondering if he would ever return. He always did. It was part of his plan, I guess.

Gradually, he started hanging out closer and closer to the house. First sprawled out in the center of the driveway, then on the porch, and, eventually, jumping on the mailbox attached to the house just outside the kitchen window. He literally was a peeping tom (cat). The first time he did it, he scared me half to death! I turned around to see a big old head staring back at me through the window.

Another day I pulled into the driveway and found him lying on his back with all four paws in the air.

"Oh no," I said to myself. "He must have gotten hit by a car and decided to crawl up on *my* porch to die!"

I got out of the car and shut the door. He didn't move. I edged closer to see if he was breathing. *Oh, Jesus*, I thought to myself, *now I'm supposed to bury random roadkill? What the heck?*

With that, this big, buff, ball of fur rolled over in my direction with a huge yawn and a look that said, "What are you looking at? What's the problem?"

I shook my head and told him, "If you want to eat, you have to let me get into the house."

Ever so slowly he got up, stretched, and let me by. He jumped up onto the mailbox and essentially said, "Hurry up, lady. I'm hungry!"

When he attempted to muscle his way into the house without having been seen by a veterinarian, we had a little chat.

"Dude, there's another cat in the house, and she's an old lady." I said to him. "I'll gladly move you in *after* you're neutered and vaccinated—and not before. You understand?"

I don't think he did because he kept trying with more and more force each time.

I made an appointment to get him vaccinated and neutered the following week. He stopped showing up for a few days. I waited. Eventually, he showed up and sat in the sphinx position at my feet. I sent him Reiki and talked with him. I explained as best I could what was going to happen with the vet's appointment and his move into the house. I hadn't even considered I hadn't been able to pet him yet, and that Sunshine was 17 years old *and* roughly one third of Boo Boo Kitty's weight.

The night before the appointment I tricked the musky male with an empty cat food can and got him into a carrier. He was confused and clearly not happy—not happy at all. The next morning, after a long drive of yowling, we arrived at the clinic.

I warned the veterinarian technicians that he was feral and, to my knowledge, had never been handled. They looked at me like I was nuts, smirked confidently, then asked, "How did you get him into the carrier then?"

"I tricked him."

The tech shrugged and turned away. I'm fairly certain there was an eye roll involved—just out of my view.

Boo emerged from the carrier warily and started to receive his rabies shot. He broke free easily and leapt from the exam table as the syringe dangled from his backside. The techs looked at me with surprise.

"I told you he's feral," I said.

Three professionals cornered him, returned him to the exam table, and finished giving the shot. He was neutered, and I picked him up later that day—still groggy.

I had no idea what I was getting myself into but knew I was willing to give this "throwaway cat" a chance to feel loved. Despite not receiving a whole lot of love from the humans I lived with growing up, I sure knew how to give it. I brought Boo into a back room of my house and tucked him in for the night in an extra-large dog crate—for now.

The first few days were terrible and stress-filled with both cats going on hunger strikes. Once we got passed that, I would sit with Boo and allow him the opportunity to interact with me on his terms. He was different inside the house, but not exactly a gentleman yet. He was pushy and forceful. I played music for him and plugged in a pheromone air freshener to calm him. Eventually, I expanded his space to two rooms, for which he was grateful.

When I introduced the two cats for the first time, it was awful. Boo lunged at Sunshine as if she was prey. Sunshine screamed. I grabbed Boo and separated them quickly! The next time, and several times after that, I had Boo in a harness and on a leash. He learned quickly how short that leash was!

I kept them separated for several months and worked with them daily. Sometimes I would switch their spaces; Sunshine would get two rooms and Boo would have the rest of the house. This mingled their scents throughout the house. I was determined to make this work! It took about a year.

During that year Boo's playfulness came out. It became clear he was just an overgrown kitten, a Baby Huey of sorts. Boo learned Sunshine was a senior and not as strong, fast, or agile as he was. He learned he had to dial it back when he played with her— waaaaay back. He contentedly jogged behind her when they played tag, careful not to outrun her. He also knew Sunshine came first. They were able to enjoy each other for over two years before Sunshine was called home.

Secretly, Sunshine taught Boo so much during that time. She taught him manners, patience, Reiki, and how to love and support me once she was gone. He absorbed everything his mentor taught him, and more.

Boo slept on my bed every night. He would snuggle for a while and then move to my feet. If I got up in the middle of the night for any reason, he accompanied me and escorted me back to bed when I finished. He never returned to bed until I was back in it. Boo was also an early riser. He sat by my face and stared at me. If I didn't open my eyes, he very gently caressed my face with his left paw. If that didn't do it, he extended his claws ever so slightly and tried again—always lovingly.

Finally, fully safe and loved, he blossomed into an amazing cat who wanted to be involved in everything. He loved jumping up on my back. I would walk around the house doing chores, and he'd be up on my shoulders the whole time. I'd turn to look at him, and he would smile and rub his face on mine. He learned how to love, and he loved loving everyone—specially the little ones who stayed over quite frequently.

I was the cool aunt—always making life fun and creating surprises. One winter weekend I told the twins we were sleeping in a tent.

They looked at each other, as all twins do, and responded in unison, "No way, Aunt Sherri, it's too cold out."

"Yes way," I said. "You know this aunt never lies."

And so it was. The tent was set up in my living room—complete with a furry foot warmer named Boo. The smile on Boo's face as he laid in wait, along with the surprise on the kids' faces, is a memory no one can ever strip away. It was such a fun weekend for all of us. Sadly, this memory remains bittersweet.

Despite growing up on the streets, Boo knew what the litterbox was instantly. That's why I found the smell of stale urine odd one day. I smelt it but could not find the source. It drove me crazy for a few days. I felt around on the floor and the carpet and was unable to feel it anywhere. But I could smell it, and it was rank! Days later I watched Boo go into the half bathroom. He jumped on the toilet and then onto the sink. I moved closer to the open bathroom door. I heard a trickle and thought, "What the heck is he doing in there?" After a minute or so, I heard him jump on the toilet seat and then down to the floor. He walked out of the bathroom with an air of confidence—relieved, his tail in its signature position of a question mark. I proceeded into the bathroom to find the source of the urine smell. Boo had trained himself to use the sink for pee-pees! I ran the sink water as if to "flush" the toilet for him. He really was the coolest cat and surprised me frequently!

By now he had left all of his fear, anger and feral tendencies far behind and had grown into a loving family member. He was going to be my last cat—or so I had thought. A feral kitten found her way into my life on Halloween in 2012. A tiny, black ball of fur was picked up near the Somerville train station and ended up at my house. Spooky has her own story in another chapter but shared part of her life with Boo.

Spooky was tiny and barely filled the palm of my hand. Boo had come so far in the years I had him, but I was still concerned about his past—especially how he had initially greeted Sunshine several years before. I was anxious as I introduced them. Spooky was safe in the extra-large crate as I talked to Boo about our new family member before the introduction. I still remember the moment I opened the door to "the nursery." It was as if Boo and I were in the maternity ward at the hospital and he was meeting his new sister for the first time. Boo sat near the door of Spooky's crate and watched her lovingly. He looked at me, then at her. I knew instantly they were going to be okay—and they were.

Boo protected Spooky and made her feel safe and loved. They were inseparable. Oh, how I would have loved an older sibling like Boo. He was kind, patient, loving, and protective—not in an overpowering way but in an "I'm right by your side" supportive way. They did just about everything together, and I loved watching it. One of my favorite pictures is of them sitting side by side in the sphinx position with Spooky only half Boo's size. They enjoyed each other for years.

One day, out of nowhere, I froze in shock as I watched Boo pee a lake on the bed. The litterboxes were clean, and the door to the half bath was open. The next day I watched him pee in the bathtub. Something was up so I made a vet appointment.

Because of his lack of good nutrition at the start of his life, he was susceptible to problems earlier than indoor cats. He was

diagnosed with a fast-moving kidney cancer. A trip to the specialized vet hospital resulted in a few very expensive treatment options without guaranteed results.

"You don't have to decide today. Take a few days to decide," they said.

Heartbreak set in. Having gone through cancer treatments myself, did I want to put my beloved Boo through it? He had to give me a sign. I gave it a few days and decided to try one of the options. He deserved a chance. Boo stopped sleeping with me. I begged him to please lay with me one last time. He was retreating. No matter how hard I tried to love on him, he pulled away. He declined quickly.

Before we were even able to begin the treatment, he was failing. A friend and I rushed him to the specialist. They said he didn't have much time. I called a vet friend of mine and asked her to please meet me at my house. I wanted Boo euthanized at home, with me and Spooky, surrounded in love. My friend took me and Boo home.

I placed a towel on the bed and laid Boo down gently. I got to lie with him one last time as we waited for the veterinarian to arrive.

"I love you, buddy. You are the best cat ever," I told him.

No longer smiling, his body giving up, I thanked him for one last cuddle session and told him it was okay.

"Go find Sunshine," I whispered.

Boo kitty, the love of my life, shook and shuddered briefly before his body went still. I kissed his head and stroked him lovingly for several minutes before the vet arrived to confirm clinically what I already knew.

This special cat was the first I'd ever had cremated. His ashes are in a beautiful box on the nightstand next to my head. I can't imagine him being anywhere else.

Even though they're no longer physically in my life, the memories of Mr. Boo and the twins I mentioned earlier have held my heart together through some very trying times. Those really good memories are the best glue ever, and for that I am eternally grateful.

Chapter 7
Spooky

"HEY!" I shouted. "What are you guys doing!?"

I was driving on a local road that runs parallel to railroad tracks. Having just left the grocery store, I was in a hurry to get home and cook for friends—but not in too much of a hurry to not notice something that didn't seem quite right. I saw two teenage boys on the incline leading up to the tracks. I whipped the car around quickly as the unusual sight registered in my brain. Before the young men had a chance to fully answer, I saw this tiny, black ball of fur scramble partway up the hill, just out of their reach.

"Uh, trying to catch this cat" was the response.

"Do you have a plan if you catch it?"

"Uh, no, lady. Do you?"

As I put my car in park, I heard myself mumble, "Oh boy, this is not going to end well. They got me."

I crossed the road and attempted to help them. This tiny kitten was the fastest I'd ever seen and clearly feral. She had absolutely no socialization or trust for humans.

"We need food," I said to the boys. "She's hungry."

I gave one of them a couple of dollars with instructions on what to get from the store across the street.

For several minutes we tried using the food as bait to capture her. She was definitely faster and more street-smart than any of us. Every time we got too close she'd scamper just out of reach. I had to leave but didn't want to leave the kitten or the boys without a backup plan.

I called a cat rescuer friend of mine. The boys kept an eye on the kitten and waited for my friend to arrive with a trap.

The trap was set up and baited while the trio gave the kitten adequate space to feel safe. Almost immediately, it entered the trap—but it didn't spring shut! She was too light to set off the closing mechanism. My friend had to act fast. She knew from experience that once the kitten was full she would take off.

My rescuer friend grabbed a nearby rock. She had one chance. If she missed, she'd spook the kitten for good! Fortunately, my friend was a former softball star. She wound up, likely said a silent prayer, and threw! BAM! The trap slammed shut!

"Brrrring," my phone rang. "We got her! Now what?" my friend asked.

"Uh, any room at your inn?" I asked.

"Nope. We're full," she replied.

"The boys?" I continued.

"They're gone already. They left as soon as she was safe."

I had flashbacks of how ugly it had been when Boo first met Sunshine—how long it took for them to get along, how I realized I still missed Sunshine terribly, and how I didn't want to set myself up to have to go through pet losses over and over again. I had made the decision so many times before that when THIS one goes, that's it. No more.

"I can't bring her into the house without being seen by a vet, and I don't have a crate to keep her in," I blurted in a panic, almost knowing what was coming next.

"We're on our way to your house. I already have a crate in the car for her. Get ready. We'll be there in 10 minutes."

Under protest, I started gathering kitten supplies. This process was creepy. It felt as if the items I needed were floating to me effortlessly—blankets, dishes, toys, and an appropriately sized aluminum tin to serve as a litterbox. Before I knew it, Spooky, who was barely as big as my hand, had arrived. After all, what else would you call a black cat that comes into your life on Halloween?

The crate was set up with "her new things," and she was situated in my garage. For a feral cat, she had been through quite the ordeal that day. I tucked her in for the night and closed the garage door. The whole experience didn't feel real; it felt far away, dreamlike.

When I woke the next day, it still didn't feel real— not until I opened the garage door and saw the crate. The crate with the tiny black ball of fur with the beautiful eyes looking back at me. That occupied crate made it real. "Oh boy," I said to myself, "now what?"

My friend arranged a vet appointment so I could move Spooky into the house as quickly as possible. She reminded me even though she was a kitten, she was a feral and *might* have rabies or something else. "Be sure to use gloves when you handle her," she said.

Having handled feral cats before, I know they can get incredibly nasty when they feel threatened. I knew to move quickly getting her into the car for her appointment. I opened the car door and had the carrier ready with its door open and prepared for Spooky's transfer from crate to carrier. I put gloves on and looked deeply into her eyes.

"We good?" I asked her. "I won't hurt you, and I promise to be gentle."

I put myself in her paws. The gloves looked big and scary so I took them off. I didn't even consider what I would have to go through IF she decided to bite me. Our eyes locked as I reached into the crate slowly while she backed herself into a corner. As soon as my hands felt the softness of her fur, there was no turning back. She found a tiny space in my heart—a space meant just for her.

Spooky saw the vet and moved into the house that day. She remained in a crate until I was sure that she knew how to use the litterbox AND that Boo would mind his manners. It wasn't long before I realized Spooky wasn't *my* kitten, she was Boo's—and together they would be my teachers.

They were inseparable. Their love for each other was out of a Hallmark movie. They ate together, played together, slept together, and sunned together. Boo's presence made Spooky feel safe, and he delighted in being her older sibling. To describe them as bookends would be an understatement.

Hindsight is amazing. It allowed me to clearly see the ripple effect of the patience, love, and understanding Boo received *from* me in his relationship with Spooky. I was humbled and honored to hold space and be Boo's catalyst for change. There was also an "aha" moment *for* me in observing how "healthy siblings" behave and treat one another. Like Spooky, I looked up to my older sibling for a long time with awe, as well as for love, protection, and guidance. Over fifty years later, with a lot of hard work and introspection, I also finally accepted that my sibling is not anything like Boo—and probably never will be. The realization and frustration of not having a healthy, supportive, loving familial relationship has been replaced with the awareness of what I *do* have. I have an amazing skill that allows me to participate in and

Photo by Greg Backman

witness healing and heartbreak in *healthy* families multiple times over. The irony is how hard I fought to hold onto the family I had, despite it not feeling good much of the time. Once I let them go completely, I immersed myself in the incredible gift I received in their place—and healing and magic began to happen.

Every time I saw one of the cats, I knew the other was close by. Boo smiled at his younger sister in a way words can't describe, and Spooky looked up to him in much the same way. It was clear she felt safe and secure with him nearby. Neither demanded much of me because they had each other until Boo passed when Spooky was four years old.

Boo was the glue that held us together. His presence drew Spooky out of hiding. Once he was gone, Spooky regressed to her feral ways. Almost always hiding, you wouldn't even know I had a cat. She'd appear for food, and there would be daily evidence that she used the litterbox, but only once a day—quietly. It was hard to say if she was mourning the loss of her big brother or just incredibly low maintenance. I couldn't tune in to her because I was caught up in my own grief. For cat's sake, I had to know.

Enter Chase.

Chapter 8
Chase

"I'm really not sure. Spooky isn't just any cat; she's a fearful feral," I said to a dear friend who raises kittens. "She started hiding again after Boo died."

"He's special—really special—and meant to be yours. I can bring him over for a playdate with Spooky."

And so she did. She brought the tiny gray tiger kitten named Chase. He was adorable and confident, born exactly five days after Boo made his way to the other side of the rainbow bridge.

It didn't go well. It didn't go well at all. Spooky pancaked. Pancaking is an extreme fear response. It is when an animal flattens themselves as much as possible in an attempt to become part of the flooring. If you try to lift them, they stiffen their bodies and "will" themselves to be deadweight. This behavior makes it more difficult to move them. She wished herself to be swallowed up into the carpet. It was heartbreaking. Spooky, who was at least four times the size of the harmless, hand-raised, bottle-fed kitten, was terrified. When I pried her off the floor and tried to comfort her, the little pads on her feet were sweating. She was shaking and panting as though she were in imminent danger. My attempts to calm and soothe her were fruitless. She was so panic-stricken she wasn't even aware of me. It was awful. My friend didn't stay long that day—and she took Chase home with her. I had to honor Spooky's fears.

I remember how fear felt. There were so many fears cast on me as a child. I had a fear of the dark, the basement, heights, water, crowds, doing something wrong, and many more. Heck, I even feared being tormented and mocked for *having* fears. None of it felt good. I held space for Spooky to process her fears of this little furry thing who invaded her house if only for a short while. Spooky and I talked it through. She was willing to try again. We'd try an overnight next time. We did, and Chase never left that second time—and boy, has it been fun!

Chase grew up with plenty of other cats around so he was quick to approach Spooky and rub his scent all over her. The look on her face told me she wasn't quite sure what to make of it. There

Photo by Greg Backman

was no hissing or fighting or roughhousing. When Spooky had enough of Chase, she would remove herself to her "safe space"—under the recliner. Chase wasn't sure what he was hiding from but followed her under there. It was actually pretty funny. Spooky quickly learned that Chase was NOT a threat. He was goofy and weird, as far as kittens go, but certainly not a threat. The two couldn't have been any more different.

Spooky likes certain people foods and goes berserk for them; Chase has absolutely no interest. Spooky likes her treats; and at first Chase did not. Spooky had a talking to with Chase and taught him how they could "work together" to get treats (or else!). They waited for the bathroom door to be opened. On Spooky's "go," they would rush in. One opens the door to the towel closet while the other jumps in on top of the towels. Once the first cat is in, the second follows, and then the closet door closes behind them. Time will not bring them out, and neither will dinner. As soon as I shake the treats, I hear one cat hit the tile floor in the bathroom and then the second. I hear Spooky say, "Good job, kid," through the satisfied crunches of her treats. And Chase? Well, he chokes them down like broccoli. It's the only thing Spooky really asks of Chase.

Spooky is quiet and rarely in my business. She observes. Chase, on the other hand, is incredibly vocal and requires near endless attention and stimulation. He is more dog-like than cat-like. He even plays fetch. He fetches plasticware, pipe cleaners, straws, and whatever else tickles his fancy for the day. He has helped me "pack" on more than one occasion. Friends have found plasticware, pipe cleaners, and straws in their gift bags. "Fetch" usually happens in the middle of the night and can go on for more than 15 minutes.

Chase can also be extremely affectionate. I've seen him groom Spooky into a deep sleep. He'll also stand on my chest and lick and nibble my nose and chin. Not just once but multiple times.

He is also an accomplished athlete. Spin class is his specialty. I've returned home to find an entire roll of toilet paper "spun" onto the floor all the way down to the cardboard holder. On days like that, Spooky reminds me, "It was YOUR idea to get another cat."

Chase can also be found playing in water—the tub, the sink, his water bowl. In fact, it took several tries before I found a water dish he couldn't tip over. Now he is content to sit in front of the water dish, dip his paw, and lick the water off of it. I can't even look at Spooky when he does it; I already know what she is saying in her head: "It was YOUR idea to get another cat."

So far (I say "so far" because their stories are far from over), they have ganged up on me a couple of times. Besides the regular treat shenanigans, there was the litterbox debacle. Spooky had hers, and Chase had his. Spooky had a pine pellet litter that broke down into sawdust over time. She's been using that litter as long as I can remember. Chase had a lightweight, compostable litter the manufacturer decided to stop making. Before I was completely "out" of Chase's litter, I started putting some of Spooky's pellets into it. The goal was to have them both using the same litter— Spooky's pellet litter, I hoped. Chase stopped using *his* litterbox. He would use Spooky's box but only when the pellets were broken down into sawdust. Spooky wasn't happy about sharing *her* litterbox with Chase. I went out and got traditional clay litter for Chase. Alas! He started using his own litterbox again, and then Spooky stopped using hers! Now they both have the clay litter— you know, the kind that makes everything in your house dusty like you just sanded sheetrock. I personally think the two cats conspired against me.

As long as they're happy, I suppose.

Chase and Spooky have shown me what a good relationship looks like. I learned from them that you can get along with others, even if you are completely different from one another. They have shown me how to have fun. They remind me to take naps, make time for play, and soak in the morning sunshine. They have taught me patience, humor, and what love looks like. Most of all, they have taught me what a family looks like—and that OUR story, the story of our healing, is just beginning.

Chapter 9
Cooper Chang

I love pushing my face into the soft fur near your neck. Inhaling deeply, I can always tell if you are freshly bathed, had a good swim recently, or rolled around in something I wouldn't have. Breathing in your scent, connecting with your energy, and being present with you fill my soul. I wrap my arms around you as my fingers disappear into your semi-curly, fluffy, Golden Retriever coat. You represent all that I long for, and much of what I've lost so far in this physical lifetime. I feel every bit of you. I hear your breath and your heartbeat. I feel your fur on my face and the warmth of your body next to mine. Your presence fills me with gratitude and love in a way words cannot describe. I want to stay here with you forever. It is a place like no other. It is cozy and safe and loving. I open my eyes. Tears flow. The burning lump of reality returns to my throat. Your physical body has been gone for years—but the beautiful memories we shared still hold a special place in my heart.

He was lying in the dirt alone by the bench in the opposing team's dugout. His front legs stretched in front of him as his head rested comfortably on top of them. He smiled as he stared out into the outfield at his person. He was the friendliest, smartest, most handsome, gentle, loving Golden Retriever I'd ever met. He was Cooper Chang.

For years, I would love on him when my team was up to bat, and we were playing his mom's team. While my teammates talked softball with each other, I talked "dog" with Cooper. We talked about what it was like to be him—loving, kind, loyal, adorable, and balanced. He was *always* ready to give and receive love and attention from whoever was around. I was inspired by Cooper's outlook on life.

I was also always respectful of "the whistle," which came from Cooper's mom when three outs were made. She dropped her glove in the outfield, and Cooper raced out and retrieved it. I was in love and in awe every single time. I hated short innings because I selfishly wanted to spend more time with Cooper. Everyone in the softball circuits knew, or at least knew of, Cooper, but not everyone knew how to talk to him. He was a special boy indeed.

Photo by Jenn Chang Hower

An opportunity came up to play in an all-day softball tournament so I took it. I had been chatting it up and rubbing on Cooper for quite a while—years, in fact.

As I loved on him, I heard a booming voice come up from behind and ask, "Who is this person that just keeps loving up on my dog?"

I turned and came face to face with Cooper's mom, Jenn. We

became fast friends and even started playing on some of the same teams. I got to spend even more and more time with Coops!

I learned so much about Golden Retrievers from Cooper. Goldens are incredibly smart and loyal; above all, they are built to please. Cooper was the perfect gentleman. He never jumped, begged, or stole food. He was the complete opposite of my psycho sibling's Golden who never received proper training. I remember the amusement my sibling found in watching the terror on her twin grandkids' faces. They were afraid of being knocked down or having food stolen right off their plates as my sibling laughed while they cried.

Coops really was perfect in every way. He was smart, handsome, loving, loyal, and so much more. He also had a strut that turned heads—human *and* animal. You couldn't look at Cooper and not smile. It was impossible. No matter what he was doing, he did it with grace and style—even aging.

When Cooper's hearing and eyesight started to fail, he could no longer come to our softball games. Whenever we played near his house, I'd go visit him. I'd bury my face in his fur and love him up as much as I could. He ate it all up. I would whisper in his ear. He didn't really have to hear me; he felt me. I could tell from his body language, smile, and ever-wagging tail. Cooper's heart was as full as mine.

I will never forget how handsome and easygoing he was. Never. I will also never forget "the call," and the last time I saw him.

"Hiiiiiii, whatya doing?" Jenn said after I answered the phone.

"Uh, talking to you," I responded.

I could hear Jenn take a deep breath on the other end of the phone. I knew it wasn't good.

"Sooooo, I thought you should know. Cooper's not doing well…and we're taking him tomorrow…and I wanted to know if you want to see him before we take him, you know, to the vet for the last time."

"I'm so sorry, Jenn. Of course I want to see him!" I said as my eyes filled with tears, my throat began to burn, my nose started running, and my heart felt heavy. The thought of life without Cooper Chang was overwhelmingly sad. Few have filled my heart as full as he—very few.

I pulled myself together and drove to Cooper's. The house was filled with a thick sadness, almost as if he was already gone and the mourning had begun. It was hard to look anyone in the eyes—Jenn, her mom, her dad, her fiancé. We all knew this day would come but we didn't want it to. We weren't ready. Not today. Not ever. Not Cooper. *Oh, please God,* I thought, *not Cooper.*

I got down on my hands and knees and leaned my face into his fur. My heart broke—for me, for Cooper, for his family. A lifetime of abuse prepared me for holding back my emotions, choking back the tears, ignoring the burning in my throat, my heart ripping apart. The lifelong fear of being mocked for actually caring about something kept my eyes dry as the desert. Meanwhile, my insides felt like a volcano ready to erupt.

I managed to push all the emotions aside to be present for Cooper and his family. They talked about how hard it was for him to get around and how it wasn't fair to keep him around in his condition. He deteriorated more each day. I tuned into Cooper and had to laugh out loud. Cooper didn't care about his failing body. To him it wasn't a big deal. I asked him what he wanted, if he was ready. His answer was that of a shoulder shrug. Through to the end, Cooper remained Cooper, charming and easygoing.

Cooper was laid to rest the following day. Almost immediately, he sent signs letting us know he had made it and was okay. He reminded me I can draw him in and connect with him anytime I want. All I have to do is close my eyes—close my eyes and imagine pushing my face into the soft fur around his neck. As I open my heart in gratitude to this gentle spirit being, the rest takes care of itself.

In life, Cooper gave me so much few will ever understand. In death, he reminded me I can connect with him nearly the same way. In between, he brought me into his family. Lucky for me, they share the same heart as Cooper.

Chapter 10
Frankie

"He's vicious and unpredictable—a liability to the shelter."

"We should probably euthanize him before the week is out—before somebody gets hurt."

"Keep him in the back."

"Only senior staff are allowed to handle him."

Those were the words I heard as I approached the shelter office.

"Who?" I asked.

In unison, the shelter staff responded, "Frankie."

"Can I see him?" I asked.

"Yep, he's in the back. Just be forewarned: He's nasty."

I was my town's appointee to our local regional animal shelter. While most appointees would just show up at board meetings and make policy decisions and pay bills, I have always been more of a hands-on person. I want to fully understand the work, the environment, and as much of an operation as I can before trying to set or enforce policy. What most people didn't know at that point is I'm also an animal communicator, empath, and healer. If anybody was going to be able to give Frankie a voice or a chance at a good life, it would have to be me. The first step was to understand where he came from.

I opened the door to "the back." Frankie was in the first kennel on the right. Immediately, he started barking ferociously and attacking the kennel gate in an attempt to get to me. My insides churned at the thought of what he could do to me if the gate failed.

It was not pretty. His lean, muscular body could have easily torn me into shreds. At the time pit bulls were receiving an incredible amount of press about how dangerous they were—all of them. Since this was my first time being so close to one, it was a little unnerving. I just stood there, as calmly as I could, as he barked and threw himself at the gate. *Frankie had a really rough start*, I thought to myself. Someone failed him big-time. It tore at my heart. Because he was clearly agitated by my presence, I didn't stay long that first day. His barking was so loud and rage filled, I doubt he even heard me say, "I'll come see you again tomorrow."

Aside from his current behavior, Frankie was the most handsome pit bull terrier I'd ever seen. He was what they call a "red." What made his looks even more striking was the white patch on his chest, right over his heart. The problem was his current rage and aggression were also the worst I'd ever seen. What could have possibly happened to make this striking dog so violent? I couldn't help but wonder what Frankie had been through. Even though his "normal" must have been terrible, it was what he knew. But now his situation was even worse, perhaps dire. *Can I really help this pup be rehabilitated?* I wondered.

I came to see Frankie the next day and the next. Each time his one-way monologue lost volume, strength, and length. My visits got longer. Over the coming days Frankie's body language started to soften as well. I showed up faithfully and listened to him. I listened as he let out the anger and frustration about his past and current situation. During these initial visits, the only time I spoke was when I started to leave, when he was finally quiet enough to hear me say, "I'll see you again tomorrow. Have a good night, Frankie."

Since my visits were getting longer, I decided to bring in a chair. Initially, I positioned it about four feet from Frankie's gate. The more he softened, the closer I got. I could see that for the first time in his life he was starting to feel safe, loved, and heard. He was finally open to the possibility of a different way of being. The true essence of Frankie's potential to love and to be loved was starting to peek through. Frankie learned that holding on to trauma, abuse, and betrayal are exhausting. As a result, he exhausted himself to the point of no longer being able to fight the love and understanding I was offering. He chose to expose his vulnerability and curiosity about receiving love. As he let go of the darkness of fear, he let in the light of love.

One day I put my chair as close to the gate as I could. Frankie came forward in his kennel. He put his head down shyly and leaned his side into the gate. He was trying to get as close to me as he possibly could. Much of the fur on the leaning side of his body poked through the chain link gate. I reached out to Frankie slowly, carefully, gently. I lovingly stroked the fur that was sticking through the gate with the back of my hand, and I told him he was safe now.

"No one will ever hurt you again," I whispered.

That was the first day I saw his bedroom eyes. I knew then he had turned the corner. There are no words to describe the feelings that washed over me in that moment. It was a beautiful feeling to experience that he willingly and completely surrendered to love. THIS was what he craved. THIS was deep down what his heart knew was possible. On this day when I prepared to leave, there were tears in my eyes, and my heart was full. "I'll see you tomorrow, Frankie. Have a good night." I believe Frankie's heart was full, too.

The next day Frankie was waiting for me with his body pressed against the kennel gate. He was filled with knowing he was loved and appreciated and safe. We made eye contact. It was the kind of eye contact that lights up your heart and fills your whole body.

I looked deeply into his soul and asked, "What happened to you? Please tell me. You're safe now."

I felt Frankie's body tense; I felt his fear, his anger, and the rage of the people around him before he found his way to the shelter. I felt an ugly scene start to take shape—people poking at him with sticks, calling him names, and yelling; then the scene went black. I witnessed Frankie touch his past, the darkness he grew up with and let go. In that moment I thought he was sparing me the gruesome details of what he endured as a pup in an abusive and dysfunctional household. I know now, years later, he was mirroring my own past—a past so painful I hadn't yet developed the skills to face it, much less deal with it.

The day had come when I had to put the fear of telling the shelter staff about my special gift with animals, for Frankie's sake. It was scary. I weighed my options. They would either be receptive, or they would laugh and ridicule and call me batshit crazy. I mustered the courage to tell the shelter staff what Frankie showed me. I also shared how much he'd changed since that first day and that I thought he deserved a chance, rather than "the needle." They agreed he had improved but insisted that if he was given a chance, we had to proceed with caution. Soon after Frankie was moved "up front" with the rest of the dogs up for adoption. He was still a "red collar" dog—only available to be walked by senior volunteers—but was moving in the right direction.

I wasn't the only one interacting with Frankie. Initially, the shelter workers took care of the basic physical needs such as food, water, kennel cleaning, and walking while I took care of his emotional needs. In time, more experienced shelter volunteers showered him with love and attention as well. He was progressing nicely, even though he had quite a way to go. He still needed to learn basic commands and manners.

I was at the shelter one day when someone yelled, "Loose dog!"

I looked up to see Frankie running toward me at breakneck speed. His face was crazed and focused. In a millisecond I realized I was the only thing between him and the open back door to freedom. I had to do something—and fast. He was closing in on me, even though he wasn't looking at me. He was focused on the door. Shelter workers were chasing behind him, making him run faster. I didn't want to use my hands and risk being bitten; that would have sealed Frankie's fate, for sure. When he got within a few feet of the narrow hallway where I was, I crouched down and braced myself for impact. Like a skilled hockey player, I checked him. That was all that was needed to slow him down. The move gave shelter workers enough time to catch up, grab him, and get him back in his kennel. After checking my underwear for stains from the ordeal, I went to his kennel.

"Dude," I said to him, "what the hell was that? We want to get you into a loving home. You can't be doing that shit."

He slunk down remorsefully and gave me his bedroom eyes as

if to say, "I'm sorry. It was fun, but it won't happen again." And it didn't.

As Frankie adjusted to the routine of shelter life, he became more relaxed, which resulted in him making more friends and moving closer to his forever home. I felt it was safe to cut down on my visits and prepare myself for the day he would get adopted. After over nine months in the shelter, Frankie finally had his gotcha day. He moved into his forever home. The ferocious dog that started shelter life with a death sentence lived out his life in a comfortable home surrounded by people who loved him. He also shared his home with another hard-to-place pup. Frankie's mom fondly told me how he slept on her neck that first night—and every night after. It was his way of protecting her and feeling safe himself. I also heard of Frankie's legacy and how, because of him, his mom started a rescue that has placed more than 3,000 other dogs like him. It is amazing how a little love and understanding given to one dog so long ago continues to ripple love out into the community years later. My heart is full. Thank you, Frankie.

Chapter 11
Rocky

His head and eyes were lowered. His tail was tucked as far up between his back legs as it could possibly go. It looked as if he was trying to make himself as small as possible, wishing the ground would just swallow him up out of sight. He was trembling with fear. Rocky's uneasiness was so palpable it was heart-wrenching. His presentation was so uncharacteristic of the way pit bull terriers were being portrayed by the media.

"Is he sick?" I asked the shelter staff.

"Nope, just terrified" was the answer. "He'll be okay."

Fight, flight, freeze, and pancake are some of the more common telltale signs that an animal suffered repetitive and serious trauma or abuse. Rocky was a cross between freeze and pancake. Rocky's extreme fear was very familiar to me as we shared the same start in life.

The shelter staff were incredibly kind to Rocky. Almost immediately, they outfitted him with a pink thunder shirt. Similar to swaddling an infant, it works by applying gentle, constant pressure over the body to calm and reduce fear and anxiety. To further reduce stress while adjusting to shelter life, he was housed in the office. It was the most compassionate choice for a dog like Rocky—to be away from the ruckus of the rest of the more confident and outspoken canine residents. The office is where I first met him and told him he was safe.

One day I was alone with Rocky. I was sitting on an office chair talking to him. It was a bit of an odd sight: this "big, bad pit bull" (as many pit bull fearers would refer to him) playing small in a girly, pink, undersized shirt. I blocked out the echo of my sibling's voice mocking one of my childhood outfits as I whispered to Rocky and tried to connect. I hated how he could be labeled by others who had limited knowledge of the breed. I hated how cruel my sibling was to me when I was afraid as a youngster. He was

simultaneously pathetic and sweet. I offered him my hand to sniff. He belly-crawled closer from the other side of the office. I continued talking to him. He just wanted what we all want: to feel safe and loved. Rocky was now at my feet, his back legs stretched behind him. For the first time I saw his little tail wag. I told him it was okay; it's safe. I'm not going to hurt you. He started to stand. He slowly and cautiously put one front paw, then the other, on each of my knees. His head was low. He edged forward as his front paws moved further up my thighs to the bend below my torso. At first I wasn't sure what he was doing. His body listed to one side as his back right leg left the floor—headed for my left knee. With a little hop, he was up in my lap.

Initially, I had mixed feelings. All I could hear was "big, bad pit bull," "vicious breed," "unpredictable," "sneaky," and "calculated." As Rocky leaned his body into mine and put his head over my right shoulder, my heart said otherwise. I wrapped my arms around his body and held him like a baby until he fell asleep. The rigidity of fear melted away from his body. His breathing was now long, slow, deep, and easy. In this stillness I could feel our hearts beating together. I was reminded we are all one. This tender moment was frozen as time seemed to stand still. It was one of the most loving moments I had ever experienced in my life.

Rocky and I were able to share a few more days like this to help build his trust and confidence in people. Sadly for me—but happily for him—he was a fast learner and adopted quickly. Even though the love affair Rocky and I shared was short-lived, he taught me so much about life, love, trusting, and being vulnerable with the right beings.

Chapter 12
My Sage: The Squirrel

I scratched frantically at the earth with my hands, but they weren't my hands. They were tiny and furry with short, sharp nails that made digging fast and easy. I was so close to the ground I could smell the damp soil, the autumn leaves. I stopped, picked up my little head, and looked around with swift, jerky motions. I scratched some more. I stood on four short legs and had a tail. I tried it out as I looked behind me and flicked it from side to side. I'm certain I was smiling. *Can we try going for a run—and climb a tree?* I said inside my head. And we did! It was fun, easy, and natural. The tree bark felt different with "these" hands. For several minutes, I was caught up in play, in another being's body. I felt my inner child's imagination and sense of wonder come alive in an amazing space where time seemed to stand completely still.

I returned to my own body for a brief moment to feel the chair beneath my body and assure myself I was safe and not completely losing it.

My thoughts shifted. *I can't believe this is happening. This is the craziest, most bizarre thing I've ever experienced in my life! It's also fun! It's incredibly fun!* During a short, guided meditation, I had stepped into a squirrel's body. I experienced firsthand what it felt like to be a squirrel. I did it during an exercise while attending my first animal communication workshop.

Being in that space—that body—I didn't want to leave. In that moment my life with squirrels changed. My life with ALL animals changed. From that moment on, every single time I saw a squirrel I felt as if they knew I had taken a ride in one of their bodies. I had earned their love and respect—and they had earned mine. To this day, every time I see a squirrel I smile and remember the day one let me take its body for a test drive.

Buzz kill. Fast-forward several years. I was struggling with the decision to leave a secure, well-paying government job I had grown to hate. I had more reasons to leave than stay. But who does that? Who retires at 48 years old? The decision was not "safe," despite feeling right for me. I changed the date on my retirement letter so many times I lost track. Conversations with friends and family had me doubting myself, my thoughts, my feelings, and my abilities—abilities I was still developing.

Enter squirrel. While standing on my side porch, I caught a glimpse of a squirrel on my garage roof. It was as if she were jumping up and down like a cheerleader at a football game. She waited until she had my full attention. I clearly heard her say, "Watch this." She was like a child wanting her parent's full attention. It was something I remembered trying for as a child but never received. Dutifully, I replied, "Okay, go ahead, sweetie. I'm watching."

"You watching?" she asked again.

"Yes, yes, I'm watching."

The squirrel ran along the ridgeline of the garage roof and took a flying leap off the end to a tree some 30 feet away. I covered my eyes with my hands and peeked through my fingers as she managed to grab the tip of a branch that seemed completely out of her reach. I gasped in horror as the branch bent dangerously vertical. The scene appeared to happen in slow motion, frame by frame. I listened for the snap of the branch or the squirrel to hit the crispy fall leaves below. I watched in disbelief, with my mouth open, as the squirrel pulled herself up the tree branch, paw over paw, as the branch slowly returned to its original position—minus a few leaves. I heard it clearly. As the squirrel was midair, she yelled, "Taaaaaake a leeeeeeeap of faaaaaaaith."

My initial thought: *I've lost it.* I went for a walk.

About ten blocks into my walk I came upon a tall, thick row of hedges on the right side of the sidewalk. I had walked past these hedges dozens of times—dozens—but never once saw *any* animal activity. Halfway down the hedges, there was a telephone pole on the left. About two steps from being even with the telephone pole, a squirrel shot from the hedges sideways. It was as if someone threw it through the hedges toward the telephone pole like a snowball. The squirrel grabbed onto the pole, scampered up just out of my reach, looked me straight in the eye, and said, "You're not crazy. Well, you might be, but did you get the message? Get out of there!"

I went into the office the very next day, changed my retirement date to April 1 (no joke), and never looked back. After 29 and a half years, I left the confines of a job I had outgrown at the suggestion of not one, but two very smart and determined squirrels. I was (and still am) humbled and grateful for their counsel.

Chapter 13
Hoarder Hell to Heaven

Naomi was ripped from the only home she knew. No conversation, no explanation, no warning. She was just removed from the house and forced to move in with a stranger. She was terrified. Where were her buddies? Where were the other 130-something cats she called family? *This is scary,* she thought. *They're not going to get me. I'll just hide until I figure something out.* And so she did. She hid—for three solid weeks!

Naomi's situation came to me as a community alert. A cat that was completely shut down and hiding in her new foster home. Truth be told, I'd be scared and hiding, too! I offered to do a distance session. It only took one. I used three modalities during Naomi's session—Reiki, Animal Communication, and Integrated Energy Therapy®.

I picked a time and settled into meditation. I called in my "team"—a collection of guides, angels, spirits, Reiki masters, and others who work in the light. I asked my ego to step aside and set an intention for the highest and best healing of all for Naomi's session. As I prepared myself "to work," I could feel the humanness leave my body. I could feel the everyday nonsense of tasks and bills and competition and judgment and fear dissolving. I mentally and emotionally entered into a warm, safe space where all things communicate. The feeling is one of completeness and perfection. It is beautiful, filled with understanding, forgiving, loving, and so much more. For a few moments I basked in this amazing feeling for myself. I prepared to connect to Naomi. With a pillow on my lap, I imagined it was Naomi lying on her side. I could feel the energy start to flow. It was tingly, warm, loving, kind, understanding, and so many other wonderful things. Once my own energy body was filled to overflowing, I could feel it travel down my arms, through my hands, and into the pillow representing Naomi.

Great, I thought to myself. *She's receptive and open to the work.* If she had not been, the energy flow would have stopped or perhaps even bounced back—to date, that's only happened to me once.

Distance work such as this encounter is an advanced technique that keeps me humbled and awestruck. The cat I was working with was some 30 miles away. The thought—*How is this even possible?*—still crosses my mind almost every time! I moved my hands around on the pillow to different spots on Naomi's body. Each of the spots represents a different emotion. The first few minutes of the session were spent gathering information. I asked the usual starter questions in my head: "Are you in any pain? What are you feeling?"

The first thing I felt from Naomi was fear—fear of the unknown. She had so many questions: "Who are you, and what do you want?" she asked.

"I'm your friend. I'm here to help," I said. I called upon my team of angels, guides, and animal helpers for assistance in gaining credibility with Naomi. Very soon into the session, I could feel Naomi's skepticism melt away into curiosity.

"Where are they?" she continued. "The others. Where are they?"

"They're all safe," I said. "They are all in homes of their own."

I went on to explain there would be no more fighting for position at the food dish, water dish, or litterbox. I could feel her confusion since living with more than 130 cats was all she knew. "They're safe," I reassured her. "I'm here now just for you. It's time to put you first."

I could relate with Naomi on many levels. She didn't know what she didn't know. She didn't know it was not normal or healthy to live in the conditions she was living. She didn't know "family" doesn't always mean forever and that "family" doesn't always have *your* best interest at heart. Some families try to keep you small and enmeshed in dysfunction. She didn't know that her first family wasn't right and that hoarding of any kind is a mental defect.

What she did know was this was her family, and she had learned to make the best of what she knew—just like I did as a child—until she had to make changes, just like I did.

Like Naomi, I didn't know what I didn't know. As a kid, I heard expressions such as "family is everything," "blood is thicker than water," "respect your elders," "children should be seen and not heard," and, my all-time favorite: "I'll give you something to cry about."

I grew up believing that everybody older than me was smarter and better equipped, despite what my gut told me. And since I wasn't supposed to be heard, I couldn't ask anyone about anything. I had to just roll with whatever was thrown my way. Even though I did my best to just stay out of everybody's way, I still grew up in complete chaos, confusion, and dysfunction. Like Naomi, I didn't understand much of what was happening to me and around me. Naomi's normal was a terrible hoarding situation. Mine was incredible dysfunction compounded by a sick and sinister older sibling.

Many animals communicate in pictures. In my mind's eye, I held pictures of Naomi and each of her feline siblings individually receiving more love, attention, understanding, treats, and care than they ever imagined. I painted pictures of getting rubs and loving pets from her new family, of people talking lovingly *with* her, not *at* her. I did my best to explain what her permanent home might look like: There may be another cat (or two) or children or people—or there may not. I was honest and told her I wasn't exactly sure what it was going to look like but promised it would be better than what she had experienced so far. I promised—and I always keep my promises.

"Please trust me, Naomi. I promise you are safe and loved," I said. For a brief moment I wished the same for myself—for my inner child who was mistreated by so many for so long. I returned to Naomi.

I did what healers call "holding space" for Naomi as she processed our conversation. My hands continued to pulse as I lovingly stroked the pillow that represented this traumatized cat. I could feel her thinking. I could feel and see her eyes moving back and forth like a Felix the Cat kitchen clock as she considered her next move. I held space and waited. I waited for her. I waited for a question, a softening, a feeling, the energy to stop flowing—something, anything.

Eventually, she asked, "What's next?"

"Trust," I responded. "Please come down and give the person looking after you a chance—a chance to get to know you so she can advocate on your behalf." After a pause, I continued. "What do you think, Naomi? It's your decision."

A few moments passed. "I'm scared," Naomi admitted.

"Sweetie, you can't hide forever," I replied. "Please try—for you, for me."

I could feel her nodding in agreement. She was a little scared of the unknown but was willing to try—for herself, for me.

"Do you feel how we're connected right now?" I asked.

She nodded again.

"You can reach out to me like this anytime you need to, you hear?" I reassured her. "I promise I'm here for you."

The last thing I said was "Good luck with your new family. The right people are right around the corner for you."

Then I tearfully disconnected. Naomi had been through so much during her childhood, just as I had. *What a lucky cat*, I thought to myself. She had an army of people take her out of an awful situation and place her into a safe home. She had me to explain what's going on to jumpstart the healing process and a loving, supportive family right around the corner searching for her.

Soon after that session I received a note from Naomi's foster mom. She told me that after the session about "a substantial change in Naomi's demeanor."

"I was able to pick up and cuddle with Naomi the day after your session," the foster mom said, then added that Naomi's move to her permanent home was uneventful. "She settled in almost overnight."

It's amazing what a little love and understanding can do for the spirit. Thank you for the lesson, Naomi. There's hope and a loving family for each of us, and it doesn't have to be the one we're born into. Trust.

As I wrote Naomi's story, I checked in, distantly. I could feel her smiling as she sits on a perch near an open window. She welcomes the summer sun on her fur as the breeze tickles her whiskers. Her contented purring tells the rest of the story. She is happy, she is home, and she is loved—just as all beings should be.

I am humbled by the experience and the lessons offered by Naomi. And I trust.

Chapter 14
Raptor Trust

"Be quiet. I don't want to startle it," I said to my fellow healer friend Chris partway through our hike.

She froze, eyes widened. She had no idea what I saw at the peak. Truth be told, I couldn't believe what I saw either. I had never been this close to one before.

It's natural for me to lead when out in nature because I see things most people would either scare away or walk right past. Today was no exception. Today, in the woods, magic happened—again.

We arrived at our destination for the hike, parked, and peed before heading toward the trailhead. The route I like to take starts with an easy downhill. It winds slightly down to a small lake with an aluminum floating dock stretched across the lake's right side. This side also offers a small beach where Canadian geese congregate to poop at will and watch the human passersby.

The walk across the aluminum dock is always noisy. You can hear the strain of the weight and movement as you cross each independently floating section. Clunky hiking boots amplify the sound. Once on the lake's opposite bank, we walk the shoreline to a dike leading to the head of multiple levels of waterfalls. A post here prominently displays three hashes, officially marking the start of the blue trail.

As we enter this stretch of paradise, everything changes. Mother Nature's playground is before us. Each season brings its own smells, feels, and magic. The first thing we hear is the sound of the closest waterfall not far from where we entered. We begin to feel our stress melt away as we are gently embraced by our beautiful surroundings. I can smell the damp earth. I scramble across huge boulders—some mossy and slippery, some covered with leaves, and others proudly standing alone at attention. The trees stand like guards welcoming our childlike sense of adventure, encouraging us to play today. There is moisture in the air that feeds the rattlesnake ferns that dance with the breeze at my feet. The air is cooler here as we approach the falls. The sound of car traffic is lovingly replaced by water from the falls as it careens its way downstream around the boulders. We spend time here, immersing ourselves in the beauty and filling our souls to overflowing.

Once we left the falls, we had a quiet, reflective, steady climb to the one and only peak on this hike: our lunch stop. As hike leader, I was ahead of Chris and caught sight of the peak before her. I couldn't believe what I saw and wanted her to have a chance to see it, too. I stopped. Turning in her direction, I put my index finger to my pursed lips to indicate a silent "shhhhh."

"Be quiet," I whispered. "I don't want to startle it."

Chris froze in her tracks, eyes widened. She had no idea what I saw at the peak. I proceeded slowly, cautiously, calmly, and settled myself into healer/animal communicator mode. I instinctively and telepathically called out to my spirit team for assistance as I moved closer. Behind me, Chris brought up the rear—but at a distance. I motioned for her to get the camera ready.

"Hey, little guy, what's going on?" I said inside my head. "You're safe. I'm not going to hurt you."

I started beaming Reiki in his direction. He yawned, a clear indicator that the Reiki is being received and starting to work. At this point I was about 10 to 15 feet from a juvenile black vulture that was clearly injured. What I wanted to know was just how badly. I held loving space for the bird and sent healing his way. I turned to see Chris snapping pictures.

"Can you believe this?" I whispered.

She nodded as I continued to work.

Several minutes in I noticed his overall demeanor had changed. He was visibly calmer and more relaxed. I like to call it being "in the zone." I moved closer and closer and closer. At this point I was five, maybe six, feet away. I was awestruck by the bird's presence and state of mind. He knew he was safe. He knew I was there to help. In my head, I explained that I wanted him to test his range of motion, then demonstrated like a game of Follow the Leader. I put my arms out like wings and asked him to stretch— and he did.

I turned to Chris and asked, "Holy cow, did you see that?"

She nodded in disbelief, with her mouth open and eyes wide. I pulled my shoulders down and stretched my neck up. The bird followed. I turned my head to the left, then to the right. The bird repeated. This went on until I ran out of things to check. "How do you feel now?" I asked. I could see and feel the vulture checking in with himself. He shook the remaining kinks out of his body,

looked at me, and said, "Pretty good."

"You ready to take a test flight? I'd like to watch," I said. And off he went.

"Holy cow," I said to Chris. "Did you see that? Did you get good pictures?"

"I hope so," she said. "I sure hope so."

I retraced my steps a week later with a different friend. As I started the climb to the peak, I sent my energy ahead to let my raptor friend know I was back to check in.

"Keep a ways back," I said to my human friend. "If he's here again, I don't want to startle him."

Just before rounding the last big rock that would put the peak in view, I heard a rustling noise coming from the underside.

"Wait there," I said to my friend. "I hear something, and I'm going around the other side to see what it is."

Much to my amazement, my raptor buddy was there with his mate. "Wow, buddy, you look like you're doing great. Thank you for letting me see you and your mate and your nest." I said with heartfelt warmth. "I won't keep you. Take care of yourself, and I'll be back again." Then we left.

Some time passed before I repeated the ritual and returned to find a family of three near the nest.

Dad bird told the youngster, "That's our friend. She won't hurt us."

"Congratulations," I said to Daddy vulture. "You've done well."

I've returned several times since those first three visits. Every time I visit I send my energy ahead to let them know I'm coming. I've lost track of how old they would be and who is who. I do know that my heart smiles when I see them all soaring high above the tree line. Thank you, black vulture, for allowing me into your family. You are beautiful, kind, and loving—as all beings should be.

Chapter 15
Owl Medicine

"What the hell?" I said to my friend Chris as the GPS took us down a creepy road that literally dead-ended next to a cemetery. "We have to get out, don't we?"

She nodded.

"Alrighty then" I said, semi-annoyed.

I gingerly got out of the car and began walking toward the cemetery with Chris not far behind. It's hard to describe how I felt. I wasn't scared, but I wasn't exactly calm either. I guess anxious would describe it. Just like you see in the movies a cool mist was hovering over the cemetery—but only over the cemetery. I didn't see anybody else, but I definitely didn't feel like we were alone either.

It didn't take long. A few steps into where the headstones were we heard the hoo hoo hoo of a great horned owl. The sound came from a distant tree line that delineated the borders of the graveyard. Just as I heard the call I looked down and saw "OWL" on a mossy old headstone. It was the only stone tilted back ever so slightly to make it easier to read, *and* it was literally right at my feet.

"You see that?" I said to Chris as I pointed to the headstone.

She nodded.

"I guess we're done here, aren't we?" I asked.

She smiled and nodded again. "Yep, you needed to collect owl medicine for your trip to Peru."

We got back in the car, and the GPS behaved normally as if

nothing ever happened.

Chris is one of my healer friends. We don't get the chance to hang out often but when we do, it's ALWAYS an adventure. We're either really close to peeing in our pants from laughing, or we look at each other in total confusion as one of us inevitably asks, "Holy moly, did you see that, too? Did that really just happen?"

Today's plan was a short training hike for my upcoming trip to Machu Picchu, and we were off to a great start! For the record, I've done this hike before—dozens of times—and my GPS has never faltered. But I was with Chris so all bets were off. "Spirit" likes messing with us—big-time.

We both love animals, have a deep connection to the earth and a wicked sense of humor, and are adventurous spirits. Sometimes we go for months and months without talking or visiting but when we get together, it's like we never missed a beat. Chris is definitely one of my favorite soul sisters. Time spent with her is healing and oh so much fun! As healers, we often deplete ourselves "giving" to others. It's so nice to spend the day with the intention to receive— to receive the bounty so freely given by animals and Mother Earth. A day out in nature always refuels our souls.

That day we walked and talked and talked and walked.

"I really hope I get a drum in Peru but the shaman lady I consulted with said I won't," I said to Chris. "She said I might get a rattle but definitely not a drum."

"Dude," said Chris, "you're so good at manifesting. Just wait and see. You'll see. If anybody's going to prove her wrong, it's you."

She trailed off, and I forgot about it—all of it—the owl, the drum, the conversation. My deepest desires were out there in the universe, and I waited.

Fast-forward several months to the Machu Picchu trip—the trip I needed "owl medicine" for. I took the trip with a different friend who also happened to be named Chris. We spent a couple of days in Cusco acclimating to the altitude, meeting the rest of the trip participants, and organizing gear. It was an exciting city rich with artifacts, architecture, culture, and colorful people. The sounds and the smells—everything was different from home.

I drank in every experience. The energy in some of the sacred spaces defied reason but felt oddly familiar. Animals also behaved differently here. For instance, the dogs were weird. All but one was running as if there was a chuck wagon convention going on. Their tails were up and their eyes were focused as they walked as fast as they could without actually breaking into a run. Their feet barely touched the pavement. Every once in a while they would take a funny little skip step like they missed a beat or something. It was weird enough seeing one dog behave this way but to see all but one doing it was just crazy. The one that didn't was just a pup and apparently hadn't learned the ropes yet.

On day three we began our Inca Trail adventure. Thoughts of "owl medicine" hung in the periphery of my daily thoughts. We hiked, and we hiked, and we hiked some more. We camped. We ate. We listened to history. We joked with each other. We hiked to Machu Picchu and Wayna Picchu. I immersed myself in the experience and expressed gratitude for being able to partake in such an adventure. For four days I waited for some big owl epiphany. I got nothing. Some really cool stuff happened with other animals—but no owl and no reason to use owl medicine.

We had a celebratory dinner before boarding the train and making our trek back to Cusco for the final day of our trip. No owl. The entire trip was amazing but I must admit I felt a little cheated. We had a little bit of time to kill before heading to the airport. I had this unexplained burning desire to swing through the center of town one last time. I had to take that one last jaunt through tourist central.

As I was admiring the majestic mountains that are the backdrop of Cusco, the conversation I had had with the shaman lady invaded my thoughts. "Will I get a drum there"? I had asked. "Absolutely not. You may get a rattle but no drum," she had said. I shrugged in disappointment and kept walking. Sadness crept in as our trip of a lifetime would soon be history. I bought a few small items as mementos of the trip but hadn't found that one really special piece. We were leaving within the hour.

As I shuffled along, replaying some of the really cool things that had happened while on the Inca Trail, I looked up to meet the eyes of someone who acknowledged me as a member of his soul family with a smile and a knowing nod. To this day, I can't put that feeling into words. It was loving and familiar on an incredibly deep level. It defied explanation. After we passed I turned around to look again but he was gone. He vanished into thin air. The dude was gone. I was slightly rattled but in a good way.

A few steps later I was guided to turn down an alley. "I've been here before," I said to Chris.

Photo by Greg Backman

"No, we weren't."

"Yes, I was—in a previous lifetime," I mumbled to myself.

As I made the turn, something or someone took over my body. My pace quickened. Things got weird fast. Despite never having been here before, I knew exactly where I was going—but I didn't feel as if I was the one controlling my steps. I turned into a store and froze. I stood there, mouth open, staring at the wall.

"This is nuts. I can't even believe this," I said to myself. "I must be dreaming."

Before me on the wall was a hand drum. It wasn't just any

hand drum; it was *my* hand drum. It was handmade by a Native American Indian man and lovingly hand-painted by his wife. It is filled with powerful sacred, healing symbols and a loving intention to heal.

Painted in brown in the background is a *chakana*, otherwise known as a sacred Andean cross. By itself it is a powerful ancient symbol filled with the values and beliefs of the Incan people. At the bottom of the *chakana* stand two clear quartz crystals. They are slightly crossed at the bottom and pointed outward. Seers would be able to see the powerful healing energy radiating from the tips of the crystals. Known as a master healing crystal, quartz is known to heal any condition. It, too, is an incredibly powerful healer by itself. In the center of the drum, appearing to fly out through the circle representing the heart in center of the *chakana,* is the owl. The "owl medicine" I picked up in a creepy cemetery during a day hike with the first Chris. She is a snowy owl, one of only a few diurnal owls, and she is prominently featured on the drum. Her eyes are fixed on me. For a nanosecond she came to life.

I could almost hear her wings as she swooped through the heart of the *chakana* in the center of the drum. As her open talons reach to pick up the quartz crystals at the bottom of the drum, her wings stretch out beyond the confines of the drum to wrap around me in a healing embrace. My family, my real soul family, is here— among the furred, finned, and feathered. And I am humbled.

Chapter 16
Pickle & Louey

It was Christmas Day 2016. I had chosen to do Christmas my own way, far away from dysfunction, so I could get out and do something different. I set out to watch the live reenactment of George Washington crossing the Delaware River. Much to my surprise, it was a huge event attracting hundreds of people on both sides of the Delaware River. I suspect since the temperature was rather mild that year folks were out in force. My choice was to view it from the New Jersey side.

Not really wanting to mingle much, I tried to stay by myself away from others. Out of nowhere, I heard a voice inside my head telling me to "go to the Pennsy side."

I ignored it.

I heard it again: "Go to the Pennsy side."

Inaudibly, I said to myself, "NO! I don't WANT to go to the Pennsy side."

But the voice continued.

Finally, in disgust with arms folded across my chest, I stomped my way down the hill toward the bridge. I must have looked like a crazy person arguing with myself for seemingly no reason. I hated being told what to do but I also know that when I listen to that little voice inside my head, magic happens.

The bridge was packed with people from end to end. Some were waiting and watching while others were actively crossing from one state to the other. About 10 feet over the bridge I saw him: a golden-colored dog with a unique, furless muzzle. He noticed me, and we started communicating—silently, the way I do with animals. His name was Pickle. I asked about his muzzle and why it didn't have fur. Was it from an accident? Did it hurt? Were his people taking good care of him?

I don't remember everything we talked about, but our conversation helped to shift my lousy mood. Animals always do. His energy and love were pure. After a few minutes I looked up to see his people looking at me weirdly (I get that often), wondering what was going on. I explained what I do, and how their dog had called to me from the other side of the bridge. The woman and young man were intrigued, the husband—not so much. I gave the family an impromptu reading, not only on the dog they had with them, but on another one that wasn't even there. As we all got ready to move on, we exchanged information. The woman, it turned out, was a small animal veterinarian and definitely wanted to stay in touch.

I mailed her a bunch of my brochures, and we tried to get together a few times but were both very busy. Time got away from us. Over three years had gone by when her name popped up in Facebook as someone I might know. I sent a friend request; she accepted. Almost immediately, she reached out to tell me she had been thinking about me—and there I was. She was struggling with the decision of whether it "was time" for her horse Louey. I checked in distantly on Louey first, and we agreed to follow up with an in-person session for good measure.

When I arrived at the stable, Louey was outside with his best (horse) friend Nifty next to him. Louey's human mom was at his side, and her son was nearby minding Nifty. As I listened to Louey's mom, I observed the energy and dynamics of the two people and the two horses. Louey's people were going to put Nifty back in his stall because he had a reputation of being a jerk when anyone got too close to Louey. I assured Nifty that I meant no harm and he could stay if he behaved himself and let me work. Nifty agreed. I repeated the conversation I had with Nifty to the humans and got to work. As I began sharing Reiki with Louey, I also "sent" to Nifty and the two humans. After all, Louey's situation affected all of them. The conversation with Louey's mom included feelings of fear, guilt, and selfishness. We spoke frankly about all of those emotions and the importance of clearing them and getting to pure love. We talked through the rawness of each of them in that moment. As we talked and worked to move through those feelings, Nifty was the perfect gentleman. He wasn't the jerk everyone said he could be. I suspect what was described as jerkiness was just him fiercely protecting his friend. His intentions were simply misunderstood. Time would certainly tell.

It's hard to make the decision of when to put your beloved pet down. You don't want them to suffer, yet you do want to give them a fair chance to recover. Louey was diagnosed with sidewinders, a neurological condition that can cause balance issues resulting in a twisted gait and listing to one side. It usually affects older horses. It is heartbreaking to watch a horse with this condition try to move around. It's similar to watching two people in a horse costume who don't have their signals straight—the back end of the horse moving one way and the front end going another. Louey's human's biggest fear was he would go down and not have the strength to get back up; fighting to get back up might cause additional problems. The fear of what *could* happen caused discomfort and unsettling thoughts. Louey's mom wanted to spare him that fate—and her own heartbreak of potentially having to watch it or not being there at all. We worked with her fears. I asked Louey. I looked deep into his eyes and soul and asked if he was "ready" and "needed assistance" to cross over. It was clear that he was not. I continued working with the quartet until all the raw emotion and doubt subsided, the energy stopped flowing, and all arrived at a place of peace and contentment. I thanked Nifty for helping to hold space. He thanked me for helping his friend and family. At the end of the session all had felt heard and understood. The energy was different. The fear and doubt were gone. It had shifted into love: pure, unconditional love.

Days later I received a text Louey had gone down. A whirlwind of emotions zipped through me in an instant. I settled myself and continued reading the text. Louey went down. He went down in the muddy pasture and was struggling to get a foothold to get up. Nifty was by his side in an instant. Louey's loving horse friend positioned himself in such a way Louey was able to stop thrashing. He gained some leverage and, eventually, righted himself— still a bit wobbly but no worse for the wear.

I wished I had had someone like Nifty to stand by me when the sibling abuse emerged from the shadows. I would have been able to "right myself" so much faster with just one friend or family member standing quietly, solidly, with me while I figured things out. Instead of having people simply listen, hold space, and allow me to experience a lifetime of emotions, I was made to feel my emotions were somehow bad or wrong. I was told to "get help," "go on medication for a while," and "get over it, it was a long time ago." One family member even asked how my truth "helps us as a family"—basically dismissing years of torture, torment, and abuse along with all the emotions that emanated from the resurfacing memories. I often wondered if my abusers were strangers, how my so-called family would have behaved? Would they have still abandoned me or would they have encouraged me to seek justice? Would they have had the desire or capacity to try and understand the long-term effects of what I endured as a child if my abusers weren't people they knew?

Family treated me like a leper and ran away like a herd of Forrest Gumps. They ran, and kept running, because of what my truth meant for them and the relationship they had with my sibling. For a good part of my life, my sibling's adult children asked why we don't get along like normal siblings. My sibling would put on a cutesy face and shrug shoulders while putting palms toward the sky pretending to be the innocent one. I, on the other hand, knew something didn't feel right but hadn't been able to figure it out. Truth be told, the therapists missed it, and I didn't even know sibling abuse was a thing! Once the answer came to light, nobody liked it. A heartfelt four-page letter I wrote to the family was signed for but never answered. Who knows if it was even read?

Friends had no idea what to do for me or how to help either. Without a Nifty to right me, I was left to thrash in the mud alone. My heart ached for understanding from somebody—anybody— during this incredibly dark time in my life. I received it from animals. What my heart knew was right, the animals proved to me over and over again. What I didn't have for myself, I humbly observed it in animals and their emotionally healthy families.

I took these as sweet signs from the universe to hold my course, to trust my heart, and, above all, to follow the animals.

IT STILL AMAZES ME how this whole story unfolded. Pickle called me into this family's life. He picked me out of a crowd of thousands to help his family and their horse—three years later. I also followed the course laid out by these horses and have a few "Nifty" friends of my own today. I am also pleased to report that Louey continues to do well almost a year later.

Yes, love prevails.

Chapter 17
Diva

I felt her sadness immediately. Her stance showed defeat, head and shoulders hanging low like someone about to kick the dirt in frustration. It was tangible and familiar. It was so familiar that I had to step back briefly to inwardly and silently reassure *my* inner child that she was safe, loved, and worthy. I pulled from my virtual toolbox to clear and center myself before proceeding with this beautiful and amazing animal. I've learned that being consumed by emotions—whether mine or a client's—interferes with the healing process. Never one to be motivated by "do as I say, not as I do," I lead by example. She felt me and watched as I let my own feelings of inadequacy go.

An important first step is to listen with an open heart. Once I cleared my own heartache, I was ready and prepared to feel hers. I reassured her and asked permission before making an energetic connection and starting to work. Instinctively, she knew why I was there. Horses are smart that way. Diva's emotion started to rise. Her bottom lip quivered. She was visibly torn between continuing to hold onto parasitic feelings of worthlessness and letting them go.

I moved in closer and met her gaze. Horses cannot see directly in front of them so I positioned myself on her left, near her head. Slightly startled, her left eye mirrored my own reflection. I looked deeply into her heart and soul as I gently and lovingly placed my hands on her. In that instant I felt an indescribable surge of energy pass through us. A beautiful and powerful connection was made.

We energetically held each other in the light, burning off years of mistreatment we had endured. I told her I was here and ready to listen to whatever she had to tell me. As I looked at Diva and my own reflection, my heart whispered, "I see you. I hear you. I feel you. You are safe and loved and so much more."

The feelings developed over time. Others slowly picked away at her and dimmed her light. She became too weak to fight it. So it became part of her core belief. Each and every time things were going good, and she felt safe, someone changed the game and pulled the rug from beneath her. The internal dialogue was in a loop and getting louder. It had to change.

Photo by Greg Backman

Diva *finally* had someone to love and care for her and treat her the way she deserved. She'd been "here" before plenty of times. This is when the proverbial horseshoe drops. It happened every time she got comfortable. Every single time her person gave her up at this point. She would find herself with a new person, a new stable, a new routine. Each time it felt like another defeat and left her more depleted than then last. She wasn't sure how many more times she could go through it.

I listened and held space for her. Things began to shift. I started sharing Diva's thoughts, concerns, and feelings with her people. They confirmed that she was moved around—a lot. Their hearts broke hearing about her sadness.

"Tell her we are her forever people," they said.

So I did.

When I first started doing Reiki on animals, the benchmark I used was three yawns for a session—three. Yawning is one way for animals (and people) to release energy blockages. (Sneezing, coughing, burping, and passing gas are other ways, but yawning proved the most common.) Energetically, we also have a "giving" and "receiving" side. Diva was so far out of balance during her first session that I spent more than half of the time sending Reiki to her "receiving" side. She had given so much of herself to others that her tank was nearly empty. Each time I tried moving to her "giving" side, I was guided to stay exactly where I was. I stayed there for over 45 minutes, and she yawned the entire time.

I could feel years and years of sadness, doubt, and worry melt away. Her eyes softened. Her body relaxed. She was ready for me to work on her other side. I made my way around and was surprised that she was still releasing, still yawning. By now she had a blissful—almost stupefied—look of someone high as a kite. We were also leaning into each other: loving, healing, and supporting one another. It is a beautiful space where all things communicate, time stands still, and we are one.

As Diva's first session drew to a close, I humbly thanked her. What happened next shocked and amazed us all. She steadied herself as she bore down on her front legs and stretched her neck. We heard the vertebrae in her neck crack—crick, crick, crick, crick—multiple times as she lifted herself up and essentially straightened out her crown. A last look into her eyes that day revealed a self-assured, more confident horse—a horse with a knowing of her newfound purpose.

Diva's second session several months later in a new barn was equally amazing. As I approached, she was standing tall, confident, and happy to see me again. I got a loving and playful nuzzle. She shared how she was so happy that THIS time when she moved, her person was still her person.

"I told you—and I do my best to keep my promises," I said.

There was some clearing and releasing but it was nothing like the first session. I was able to move around without having to stay in one spot for too long. I worked with her for about 45 minutes before she backed up and shifted her body, creating an energetic triangle between me, her, and a nearby horse in a stall.

"What's up girl?" I asked.

We all saw it. She pointed her head in the direction of the other horse.

"You want to share the rest of your session?"

Her response was a nod with a snort—an undeniable "yes," even for someone who doesn't communicate with animals!

And so it was. Diva and I spent the rest of *her* session time sending healing to one of her stablemates.

Diva's third session was more of a friendly visit than a session. I was subtly drawn to her and wasn't entirely sure why. I thought it was because I needed to be in her energy again before writing her story. At least that's what I told myself and her owner. When I got there, her energy was a little bit "off."

"What's going on girl?" I asked.

She gave me a little bit of a cold shoulder.

"Please tell me," I pressed. "What's up?"

"Things are weird, people are weird, and my person hasn't been around as much. Something doesn't feel right."

COVID! Everybody *BUT* Diva knew COVID changed things for people. I relayed the information to Diva's mom, and she confirmed that she hadn't been able to be around as much. Diva felt it, and we all felt terrible.

I explained to Diva that no one knew COVID would happen and apologized that we didn't communicate the big changes with her.

"We're so sorry, Diva, so, so, sorry." I told her.

She asked me to move in closer so I did. I looked into her left eye and energetically attached my heart to hers so she could feel I was genuinely sorry. While still connected, I told her she could reach out to me anytime.

"You know how to communicate with me now. I will always answer."

She nodded, we nuzzled, and she kissed my cheek.

I was humbled by the faith and trust she and her family put in my work—work that continues to awe and inspire me. Now forever connected, I love you Diva.

Photo by Greg Backman

Chapter 18
For the Love of Jack

I hadn't worn the shirt in a while, but on this day I chose it. The black, long-sleeved t-shirt had a hole in the armpit and two holes in the left forearm made from the bite of a dog I loved. Since Mother Nature was in between seasons, I was in between long-sleeved tees and short-sleeved tees throughout the day. As I sported my three-holed shirt two days in a row, I thought this was the time I was going to actually wear it and then toss it. At the end of day two it went in the hamper. I couldn't toss it but didn't immediately know why.

Jack and his dog brother Apollo were my friend's dogs. Apollo, a goofy boxer, and Jack, a huge German shepherd with a unique personality, were dog sitting clients for about a year and a half. I remember the first day I went to the house. The key was to be in the mailbox. I had only been to the house once before and didn't remember it looking like this. I fished around in the mailbox for a key but there was none. I pulled out mail, and it was not addressed to the right person. I texted my friend and found I was on the wrong block, thanks to a typo in the house number. I made it to the right house and stood outside the front door, a little unnerved. I wasn't so concerned about Apollo; he spooked easily. But Jack's reputation was that he was unpredictable.

I stood at the door and told them, "Aunt Sherri's here. I'm coming in to let you out, okay?"

As I put the key in the lock, I heard Jack's deep bark. What had I been thinking taking this job? Oh well, I was there now.

I summoned the courage of my dead dad—a mailman who had survived multiple dog bites during his career—and opened the door.

Apollo had a look of confusion (I came to understand that's just his look), and I wasn't really sure how to read Jack. Neither dog growled or lunged at the door so I made my entrance. We stood there and looked at each other for a few moments before I asked the question every dog knows: "Who wants to go outside?"

Apollo wiggled his back half until it nearly passed his front, and for the first time Jack smiled at me from deep within his soul. His body language was confident, flirtatious, and playful—all at the same time. I was going to love this job!

The boys went outside and did their business while I stood on the back deck. I learned that Jack was a circle pooper. He would walk in circles until he found just the right spot, begin the squat, and take a few steps while he went. When he finished, he had a boyish look of accomplishment, followed by his backyard strut and confident "I'm ready for a bone" leap back up on the deck. On most days he would saunter back into the house for his treat.

There were two exceptions.

The first time was what we eventually started to call "spa day." Jack trained me slowly. He would sit while I gently brushed his head, neck, and chest—watching and waiting for just the right moment to suck me in. And then it would happen—almost in slow motion. He would lovingly lock eyes with me and ease himself down ever so slowly. Head back, belly up, with the top section of his paws bent over his chest begging for a full body rubdown. Now down on my hands and knees like a servant, I gently start rubbing only to be met with a growl. The first time it scared the crap out of me. I came to understand that growl was the sound of Jack in total bliss, his sound of total surrender.

The second time was when there was snow. Jack loved, loved, loved the snow. He loved being out in it and watching it fall but most of all loved rolling all around in it. On those days I would have to work a little harder to get him back in the house. There are no words to describe Jack's joy on those snow-filled days. It was something you could only feel with your heart. I continue to smile just thinking about how happy it made him. I learned much from

Jack about being present and enjoying simple pleasures.

I remember one such snow day very well. There was snow, then freezing rain, and then more snow. Jack knew it was snowing and was eagerly waiting my arrival. Apollo was, well, Apollo. I opened the slider to the deck, and Jack flew off it like Superman into the crunchy top layer. I didn't know it at the time but he snapped his nail down below the nail bed. I was busy washing and refilling their water bowl. I let them back in and got their treats. When I turned around to give them their bones, I noticed that the kitchen floor looked like a crime scene. There was blood all over. A quick scan of their frosty bodies led me to Jack's back toenail. Cool and laid back, Jack didn't care—after all, it was snowing. I stayed until the blood flow stopped and reported to Jack's dad.

Everything about Jack reeked of cool just as everything about Apollo was goofy. Their personalities were so different but they were so much fun. I treasured each and every day I had with "the boys" because I knew this job was temporary.

Enter Finn. Finn was a pit puppy full of energy and curiosity, a brindle with a white streak running between his eyes, down his nose, and to the sides of his muzzle. He was rescued from a high kill shelter at the 11th hour. Finn was to be crated until potty trained and closer in size to Jack and Apollo.

"They're fine together, but just keep an eye on Jack," I was told.

"Uh, okay," I said.

The very first day I had all three I entered the house and let the two big dogs out in the back yard. I went back inside to see this new little face peering out of what looked like a doggie jail. I opened the crate, picked Finn up, kissed him on the head, and carried him out back to be with the other two. Apollo was off being goofy Apollo, and Jack was sauntering around being cool. I put Finn down to do his business, and he immediately ran toward Jack. My thoughts flashed to how quickly this could go bad—especially given the size difference. I got between them just as Jack was about to give Finn a lesson. Fortunately, my forearm got the lesson meant for Finn. I felt the familiar warmth of a bite and noticed two new rips in the shirt sleeve. I wasn't ready to pull up the sleeve to get a better look.

Finn and I went in the front yard for him to do his business. It's where he would do his business until he learned his place and grew into a body fast enough to get away from trouble or big enough to defend himself. In fairness, Jack was much older and not sure how he felt about his new apprentice. Clearly, Apollo was not the teacher here.

I took care of Finn, straightened up his cell, and tucked him back in before letting the big dogs back in. Everybody got their bones, and I left. On the drive home I pulled up my sleeve. Much to my delight, the shirt looked worse than my arm. The skin wasn't broken so much; it was more of a pinch bite. I suspect that once Jack realized it was my arm and not Finn's, he released quickly.

For months the new routine was to let big dogs out back. Let Finn out of doggy jail; get him to sit for the leash and go out front to do his business. We worked on basic commands, his manners, and consistency. He taught me how smart he was—and funny. During this time Jack didn't have as many spa days because Finn required more of my time. Looking back, it didn't really take long before I was comfortable letting all three out back together.

Cool Jack went back and forth between actually enjoying having a little brother to teach and torment, and pretending not to. I would regularly catch them having fun together, and then Jack would pretend he was really annoyed with Finn. Finn had more speed and agility than the other two; Jack had the brains, and Apollo was, well, Apollo. I do believe Finn had a positive effect on Jack. He helped Jack bring out his "inner puppy" from time to time. Now that the pack was worked out, Jack's spa days returned.

On spa days Finn would torment Apollo, dazzling him with his speed and agility, and Jack would enjoy getting his rubdown and brushing. I felt accomplished on spa days, too, leaving the yard completely littered with Jack's fur. He had the thickest, most abundant coat I'd ever seen on a German shepherd, and he wore it well.

As I reflect on my time with "the boys," I remember I was going through a very dark time in my life. I was grieving the loss of three very special children. On some days the grief was so bad that the only reason I would get out of bed was to tend to the pups. They soothed my soul and worked hard to mend my aching heart.

As I made my way to sturdier ground emotionally, the boys' daddy let me know he was looking for a house with a bigger yard, closer to his work. Soon they would be moving. During this time I stayed longer, took pictures, and showered them with even more love (and bones). I cried like a baby on the last day, and all the way home.

For weeks I was lost without them and would spontaneously burst into tears. I came to realize the loss of the boys was very similar to the one they had helped me through. This feeling of loss

was familiarly painful to my heart. I tried to keep busy and, eventually, adjusted to my new normal without them. I reached out to their daddy from time to time but knew he was busy with a life that now included a new house, wife, and baby. I often thought about the boys and smiled, the love and appreciation for the time with them still palpable in my heart.

The boys had moved 16 months earlier. I hadn't worn the shirt in quite a while, but on this day I chose it. The black long-sleeved tee with the hole in the armpit and two holes in the left forearm made from the bite of a dog I loved. Since Mother Nature was in between seasons, I was in between long-sleeved tees and short-sleeved tees throughout the day. As I sported my three-holed shirt two days in a row, I thought this was the time I was going to actually wear it and then toss it. At the end of day two, it went in the hamper.

On day three the boys' doggy daddy informed me Jack was gone. It happened quickly, and there was nothing they could do. My deep connection to animals does not allow the shirt choice to be chalked up to coincidence. For the love of Jack I won't ever toss it. I know without a shadow of a doubt his spirit blew through to say goodbye and thank me for the spa days. I will continue to wear it as I have since the day the shirt was changed. I will lovingly look down at the two holes in the sleeve and the tiny scar on my forearm and feel Jack in my heart. I will close my eyes and feel his fur between my fingers, see his loving smile and bedroom eyes, and hear his blissful spa day growl.

For the love of Jack.

Chapter 19
A Special Spaniel Named Duke

I came to meet Duke by chance—or was it? His mom did a Google search on "Animal Reiki near me"—and I popped up. We exchanged information and set up Duke's first session. Upon arrival, this 14 and a half-year-old gentle Spaniel giant could not sit, stand, or walk without assistance. Despite the limited mobility, his disposition and spirit were completely content, and his heart was bursting with love. At the end of Duke's first Reiki session, he was sitting up tall—proudly—on his own and smiling.

Duke's second session was five days later. He was definitely in better shape than the first time I saw him, but he also had a ways to go. He settled in quickly and let me go to work. At the completion of his second session, he was definitely more mobile and even more content. In fact, he did his best to walk me to the door when our work was complete. I brought my camera to Duke's third session (10 days since the last one) because I somehow knew he was going to greet me at the door. Sure enough, when I pulled up, his mom opened the door, and there he was, wearing his signature smile—a smile that could melt the coldest of hearts. His body language also let me know he was pretty proud of his progress and was so very happy to see me. Truth be told, I was just as happy to see him. I believed he had turned the corner.

During our sessions I learned so much about Duke and his family. Family members told story after story about some of his adventures and favorite people. He loved his Grammy Irene, who had passed away about a year earlier. Duke was the only dog she would ever allow in her house, and they had an incredible bond. He especially loved the mirror in her dining room. The family wasn't sure if he thought his reflection was another dog or if he just really liked looking at himself. They also told of how he had gotten out a couple of times in his younger years and how difficult it was to catch him. Once was on vacation while they were at the

Photo by Nicole Huber

beach. He was supposed to be convalescing after surgery but a careless maintenance man assisted with Duke's escape. The family never told of Duke's smile on those days, but I'm quite sure it was there—and he was ever so proud of himself.

At about the four-week mark Duke wasn't showing much interest in food. A trip to the vet was cause for concern. His kidney levels were elevated, and he was put on medication. Our sessions became more frequent and were sometimes even performed distantly. Some days were better than others but each one was filled with concern for this special Spaniel. We would laugh and sometimes cry during our sessions. He continued to feel content, despite sometimes requiring coaxing to take nourishment and to have to be carried out for potty. Duke's family continued to give him the best of care and loving support while questioning whether they were being selfish keeping him around. They did not want to let their boy go, yet they did not want to see him suffer. They wanted to give him a chance to turn this thing around. For three weeks they celebrated successes and had their hearts torn out on rough days. And through it all this special Spaniel smiled—until the day he didn't.

I remember Duke's last Reiki session. He stood up as best he could, wobbled over to me, put his head on the inside bend of my elbow, and flopped into me like a baby. I held him like that as the Reiki flowed through me into him. I stayed in that position as my legs and arms fell asleep. I silently begged for a sign—a clear sign—that he was ready. I wanted desperately to be able to give his loving, devoted family the peace of mind every pet lover desires. It was another session when Duke's family opened their hearts and shared Duke stories with me. We laughed and cried and supported this special Spaniel named Duke, who taught us all so much about being present these last several weeks. As the session ended I choked back tears when I kissed Duke on the head for what would be the last time. I hugged each member of Duke's family and reassured them that whatever they decided, they couldn't get it wrong. And I left.

I received a text later that day that the family decided "today" was the day. They didn't have a time yet because they were waiting on a call back from the vet. I kept asking—hoping, begging—for a clear sign to be able to give this special Spaniel's family the peace they deserve. Hours later, I received another text that the vet was at the house. We were at the 11th hour. Duke's mom had never been through this and didn't know what to expect. I did my best to text back an explanation of how it should happen. Like any pet lover in this position, there's always that dark shadow of doubt. Here I was miles away, a passenger in a car, and it came—the sign that was sent from this special Spaniel named

Duke. It was literally a sign, a sign you could not mistake for coincidence. Framing the building's roof was a band of bright red neon lights. In fancy golden letters above the entrance, it read: DUKE'S. Slightly below that it read: Bar & Grille. He was ready!

Tears flowed as I text messaged Duke's mom that I had received the sign. I thanked my guides as tears continued down my face and a burning lump of love filled my throat. This special Spaniel has astonished and humbled me from the first day we met. My emotions were as raw as they were the day I wrote his story almost three weeks later.

I received a text sometime later that Duke was at peace.

I could feel the entire family's sorrow and love through each letter of that brief text. In my mind, I could hear the sobbing, the sniffling, and the breaking of hearts. The tears, the burning lump in my throat, they returned. This special Spaniel has touched so many, so deeply. Soon he will be reunited with Grammy Irene and so many other wonderful pets on the other side of the rainbow bridge.

My work was not yet complete. I needed to know he "made

it." I needed to know he was safe and okay and smiling that special Duke smile. I put it out there to my guides, the universe, Duke's spirit: Please send me a sign.

The very next morning I started with a cup of tea and resumed a game of Words With Friends. It's an online game similar to Scrabble in which players take turns playing intersecting words from a rack of seven letters until someone runs out of letters.

The turns went like this. "Attendees" was already vertically on the board. "Sunlit" was played by my opponent using the "s" in "attendees," and I added "heaven" using the second to the last "e" in attendees. The letters "up" remained on my board. The sign couldn't be any clearer from our special Spaniel. He made it! Again, tears flowed. I immediately sent off a screenshot to Duke's mom to let her know he made it and was safe. The signs continued.

Hours later, while shopping, I spotted a heart off in the distance. As I focused, I noticed the heart was moving. I picked up the pace to get a better look. It was the "business" end of a Rottweiler. His butt right below his stubby tail had a tan heart-shaped spot! I moved around to the front of the dog, asked permission to say "hi" from the owner, and got down on my hands and knees. This confident Rottie walked over and put his head on the inside bend of my elbow—just like Duke did that last day—and leaned into me. His owner remarked he didn't usually greet people like that and that I must have met him before. I assured her I had not. In that moment my aching heart felt a familiar tug from the "other side"—from the special Spaniel we called Duke.

The very next day while traveling from Pennsylvania to New Jersey on a stretch of Interstate 78 I've traveled dozens of times, I spotted (for the first time) a green real estate sign: Duke Realty. When I asked out loud if that was for real, I immediately saw an overpass with a sign that read: Biddle Road. Biddle is the name of a cat client of mine who passed away over two years earlier! I frequently ask animals on the other side to "receive" the new ones crossing over. To reiterate, I have traveled this stretch of Interstate 78 dozens of times and NEVER ONCE did I notice the Duke or Biddle signs before—not until I asked for signs from Duke, clear signs.

We are still not done. Duke wanted to make sure I got the

signs. I have a birdfeeder in my yard, not because I'm some great birder but because the squirrel activity brings entertainment to my two indoor cats. Because the squirrels frequently hang upside down trying to shake out the sunflower seeds, we rarely see birds there. When we do, they're not very colorful or rare. I had this burning desire to look outside one day after Duke passed and, sure enough, I saw the brightest, biggest, most beautiful cardinal just hanging out on the birdfeeder looking at my house—literally, looking back at me. We looked at each other for a little while. I know it was yet another sign from Duke.

Another day while driving I wondered how Duke's mom was doing. As the thought entered my mind, I looked over and spotted a new sign: Duke's Pet Den Pet Food & Supplies. It appeared out of nowhere, instantaneously. I was in a rush and didn't have my camera with me; I vowed to return another time. When I did, there was no on-street parking; apparently, it was "court" night because the police lot was almost completely full. There was one lonely spot left. It was on the end within perfect viewing distance from Duke's Pet Den. Thanks for holding the spot, Duke!

With every sighting I would text Duke's mom with the intention of bringing peace and reassurance that Duke was, in fact, "okay" on the other side. Eventually, she expressed concern that if Duke was giving *me* signs, then he wouldn't be able to give his family signs. I explained that simply was not true. It has been my experience that spirits can be in multiple places simultaneously so to be patient. What happened next was astounding.

I was walking on a towpath not far from my house. I was about one and a half miles into my walk when I looked up and saw a family of four walking a dog. They were still quite a distance away so I couldn't really tell what kind of dog. As we got closer to one another, I could see it was a Spaniel, the same color as Duke. When we were head-on, I had to stop, kneel, and say hello. I tried to hide my sorrow under the brim of my baseball cap in front of this couple and their two young children. I could feel the burning lump return to my throat as this unknown Spaniel proceeded to put his head into the crook of my elbow and lean into me the way Duke did for the last time exactly eight days earlier. Unable to hide my tears, I told the couple that their dog reminded me of a very special dog that left the earth eight days ago. Out of curiosity, I asked them what their dog's name was. No surprise: His name was Duke!

I dutifully and lovingly reached out to Duke's mom about my latest Duke "coincidence." She replied with an astounding story of her own that happened simultaneously to my towpath encounter. Duke answered his mom's prayers for a sign of her own AND gave me one simultaneously! She was in an antique store several miles from where I was and came upon a picture. Not just any picture. It was a picture of a Spaniel in a chair with his reflection in a mirror and XOXO on a heart nametag. This very special Spaniel named Duke saved the very biggest and undeniable sign for his mom. He giftwrapped it with a message of love and thanks and roses for a great life and the most peaceful, loving passing a dog could ever hope for. We are still not done.

There comes a time when anyone who has ever loved and lost a pet faces; the house hasn't been the same. It feels empty and quiet. There's a terrible heartache begging to be soothed. Time spent with your critter is now filled with grief and sadness. How do you move on? Guilt washes over every time the thought of "replacing" your fur baby surfaces. It's as though you are somehow cheating on them, dismissing all the special memories and love you shared. The truth is that thought CAME from your deceased fur baby. They know they can't be replaced but also know your heart. They know your heart has much more loving to do, and then they help. From the other side of the rainbow bridge, they make things happen. They put thoughts in your head and put just the right fur baby in your path at just the right time. It may even share the same name at the shelter or rescue—just in case you had a shred of doubt how to proceed. This is the case with Zeus, known at the shelter as Duke. As with all great dogs in spirit, the torch was passed to his successor. Welcome, Zeus! You hit the jackpot with your new family.

Duke's mom captured the exact moment Duke passed the torch to Zeus. Zeus was sitting in front of a china closet, looking up lovingly and attentively at a photo album. It was Duke's photo album. For a brief moment the photo of Duke on the cover came alive. The photo captured Zeus listening to Duke tell him, "It's up to you now. Keep them safe, keep them happy, and love them—and they will do the same for you."

There are no coincidences. Duke and his family came into my life at the perfect time. The love and support I felt in Duke's home is the love and support every being on earth should experience. It's

Photo by Nicole Huber

the kind of love my heart always knew was possible.

A very special thank you to Duke and his family for the honor of holding space for you and with you during Duke's transition over the rainbow bridge. Your family is the benchmark of my dreams.

Chapter 20
Charlie's Stretch: The Observer

I have found animals are way smarter than I could ever hope to be. They have led me, followed me, taught me, and supported me in ways I have been trying to express through stories in this book. Our unspoken bond warms my heart, even on the worst days. Their very presence brings me and others comfort. Even when they are not seen, heard, or acknowledged, they are in service working, healing. On this day I was neither the teacher nor student but the observer.

On the Delaware and Raritan Canal Towpath between Manville and Millstone in New Jersey, there is a lovingly placed bench in memory of a young person named Charlie Schulz. Personally knowing Charlie as an animal lover and advocate, I've come to expect magic and transformation in the area around the spillway that I affectionately refer to as "Charlie's Stretch."

On today's walk I came to the realization that Charlie's bench is an anchor point—probably one of many. It is an anchor point for healing and love. Animal magic doesn't just happen at this special bench with its aura of golden light but also along the towpath stretching in both directions from Manville to Millstone.

As I started my walk from the Manville side one morning, I was greeted by an array of different birds. I saw the most vibrant of blue jays and cardinals saw and heard the busiest of woodpeckers and robins. On both ends I could smell the faint aroma of fox that had recently passed by. I spied a lone groundhog, several squirrels, turtles, ducks, and geese as well. I saw recent evidence of beaver activity on the bases of trees and in a patch of mud at the landing zone of one of their chutes on the river side of the towpath. On the return trip I was joined by the prints of a lone deer who had crossed the path left to right and then disappeared into the grass at some point. Each one of these animals had a message and a job to do. Each was working independently, lovingly, quietly, in service to the whole—the greater good. Several times I paused to feel it

Photo by Greg Backman

and observe how the animals went about their healing work.

All but one person greeted me pleasantly with a smile and hello that day. This one woman passed by with an absent look on her way toward Charlie's bench. After we passed I looked up to see a flock of turkey vultures hanging out like sentries in the highest branches of an old tree. I heard them say, "Don't worry.

We've got her—just like we had YOU after the special Spaniel named Duke died." I smiled inside knowing what would come next.

Many people are creeped out by vultures because they think they represent evil and death. On the contrary, they are incredibly smart and represented beautifully in all the animal totem books I have read. I nodded to the vultures as I passed—something akin to "Namaste"—as an expression of gratitude for what they were about to do. My heart knew they would work with Charlie's spirit and the rest of the animals to clean up that woman's thoughts and aching heart. My heart also knew on this day love was quiet and patient and abundant on Charlie's Stretch.

Chapter 21
Peepers

The kayak launch was eerily quiet when we arrived. I had a weird feeling we weren't alone, though. A quick scan of the area revealed a small, dark mound of what appeared to be fur floating around a slight bend that led to an inlet. I walked the 20 or so feet back to the car to unload the kayak.

"Peep, peep, peep, peep, peep, peep."

The noise of our arrival must have woken her.

"Awww," I said out loud as I located the source of the cries.

Before my eyes was the tiniest of ducklings frantically circling and crying out.

"You're adorable," I said to her "and so tiny."

Then I continued to gather the rest of my gear for the maiden voyage of a free kayak. Torn as to where to put my attention, my thoughts shifted back to testing the kayak.

My friend Val shoved me and the kayak off shore into the lazily moving river. I paddled a little upstream and downstream before moving in closer to the duckling. I know normal duck behavior. I know it's not normal for a duckling to be alone. It's also absolutely *not normal* to abandon a family member. In the past I've seen mamma ducks literally count her ducklings before, during, and after a family paddle. I moved the kayak in behind the duckling to force it closer to shore. Even though it was so tiny, instinct kicked in, and it moved away quickly. I was amazed at how it water-surfed toward the shore to escape my kayak. It stopped peeping. Survival said: "Be quiet. Be still. That's not your family."

I paddled a little more upstream and down before docking and giving Val a turn. We switched positions. She became the kayak tester, and I watched Peepers. She was quietly preening and cleaning on shore, behaving as ducks do.

As Val paddled out of sight, I connected with the duckling. She was not an ugly duckling; she was absolutely beautiful. Being so little and afraid, communicating with her was challenging. *This is really odd,* I thought. *Why is there only one? Where are your siblings? Where is your mother? Are you okay?* I looked around for others. There were none. We were definitely there long enough so that if there *were* others, they would have shown up by now. Part of me felt terrible, and another part of me was content. My soul smiled, knowing this timely encounter held a deeper meaning for me.

The thought—*What kind of family would abandon one of their own?*—crossed my mind, and I chuckled. The chuckle was a clear sign of what's *really* going on here. I am being given a distraction and opportunity on the weekend of a formerly close family member's 40th birthday. The chuckle represents how far I've come in the healing journey of being abandoned by my own family. Little Peepers and I—we are kindred spirits.

In that moment I connected with that duckling on a level too deep for words. I understood the pain of being abandoned by family during the darkest hour, and the fear of being alone. I also witnessed the will to survive. After a brief rest the duckling resumed paddling frantically in circles.

I behaved similarly when my own family initially abandoned me after I delivered the painful truth about another family member. I went in circles trying to understand why family and close friends pulled away and then completely vanished from my life. It was devastating to feel like the bad guy, knowing I was the victim of repeated torture and abuse at the hands of an older sibling. Like the duckling, I had spun frantically in circles wondering if I was going to drown or be alone in the darkness forever. In those moments on the shore I saw clearly how far I'd come in my personal journey. The overarching depression and pain of being alone on holidays and special events were gone. I no longer felt anxiety on days leading up to birthdays and holidays, not knowing how I would spend them. I created new traditions that warmed my heart and fed my soul on those days.

Spinning and spinning, faster and faster, I saw it. In that moment with the duckling, I saw where I was. The dysfunctional family I grew up with put me there and held me captive until I decided to stop spinning and take a different path. My blood family—the people who were supposed to love, protect, and care for me—failed me. The truth is they are all still spinning in dysfunction, and I have chosen a different path—the path of a healer.

I started reaching out to my "chosen family." The loving, helpful, authentic, supportive people I now call family. The first call I made went unanswered. The second call wasn't exactly favorable for Peepers—it resulted in a "let nature take its course" response that didn't feel quite right to me. The third call was a charm. I reached a friend who knows all about beating the odds; one of his children has ongoing medical issues. He was there in a flash with a net and a box. We easily led Peepers into the box. I don't know how she knew we were there to help, but she did. I also wasn't sure what the next step was, but I knew it didn't feel

right to abandon Peepers. I maintained my center and tuned in to my inner guidance system for the next right step.

Since it was a holiday weekend, two calls to wildlife rehabilitators went to voicemail. The third call—to another friend with a reputation for saving animals others would euthanize—was a success! I explained the situation and asked if she would give Peepers a chance. My timing was perfect, and she agreed to care for the abandoned duckling.

By the time we arrived, a nice warm space was set up, and there was food waiting for her. Peepers ate like a champ. I thanked my friend for agreeing to help out on such short notice. Our eyes met intensely, and our hearts connected. Without a word, my friend and I had a brief but deep soul connection and understanding. However things ended up working out, Peepers was going to feel loved and supported by many—just as all beings should feel.

Dear Peepers, I may not share your bloodline, but my chosen family and I definitely had your back. Thank you for the opportunity to show you what real love feels like—*and* for the wonderful lessons you taught me in the process.

Chapter 22
Sacred Winged Initiation

I sense them before I see them. I feel them in my core before I hear them. Their energy is always ahead of their sound or their physical form: animals. Any animals, all animals. I am them, and they are me. And we are one.

I round the corner of the reservoir and the feeling is there. In the stillness there is life. I can't see it, but I feel it. I know it is here. I continue to paddle slowly, methodically, as my kayak moves gently through the water, barely creating a ripple. There is darkness at the far end. The trees that shade the water appear upside down in the water's reflection. I move forward slowly as I search for movement and listen for sounds. It is eerily quiet. The only sound I hear is an occasional trickle from my paddle's edge. My kayak lists to one side as it stumbles over a submerged tree stump. A split second of panic rose and fell with a sudden, unexpected jolt.

"Oh wow!" I whisper to myself as I spy the first one perched atop a tree stump rising just above the water a few feet. It is as still as a statue. I watch to see if it turns its head to follow my movement. It does not.

I see the next one and the next and the next. Most are on tree stumps sticking out of the water at different heights. A few are floating lazily while others have their wings stretched out in my direction. It feels like a warm, sacred welcome—a formal initiation into their world, if you will. I am sure Peepers had something to do with this.

I am seen, appreciated, revered, and loved by a gathering of more than three dozen cormorants. They are as calm with my presence as I am with theirs. I am awestruck to be so close. I thank them for the beautiful welcome and for sharing their energy and medicine. I vow to look up their message when I get home. For now, I immerse myself in the moment. All is as it should be.

I soak it in. The gentle breeze, the fleeting clouds, the peace and serenity in this corner of the reservoir. They are mine to share with these gentle creatures. I appreciate and absorb this moment of perfection, my initiation into yet another circle of beings. I feel their energy course through my core. I welcome it. I am whole.

I feel an energetic shift and instinctively know it's time for takeoff. I hear the distant splashing as some begin their ascent. The paddling and flight are smooth and graceful but the space between the two is awkward—just like life, just like change. I watch a few take off. I listen to the transition from frantic splashing to the near silent "whoosh whoosh whoosh whoosh" of their flapping wings. It is time for me to take off, too. It is time for me to spread my wings and fly like the cormorant.

With the support of the finned, furred, and feathered, I am ready. I am here. I am the person I've searched for during a good part of my life.

Chapter 23
From Fear to Friendship to Folly

"What if they mess up and never walk again? There are things I've never done that I want to do now in case that happens." I said to the guy I tried dating—back in my 20s—long before I knew I could talk to animals and long before I swore off men. "Horseback riding, I want to try horseback riding. I want the biggest, fastest horse they have." And so we went before my scheduled knee surgery.

We arrived at a local stable, and I immediately felt inadequate and unprepared. I had never really been around horses, much less actually mount and try to ride one. The guy I was dating? Yeah, he jumped on his horse like a seasoned rancher and rode off into the sunset without me. The people at the stable assumed I knew what I was doing and pointed to a horse for me to go and "fetch." I didn't have a clue what to untie, what to grab, or how to "walk" the horse over to where I was supposed to get on it. I stood there feeling stupid and mumbled to myself. The horse looked at me sideways and grinned—he was going to have fun with me.

Annoyed, a worker untied the horse and walked us over to an area where I climbed onto his back.

Holy crap, I thought. *This is a lot higher and scarier than I thought it was going to be—and we haven't even moved!*

I don't remember getting any instructions or maybe I was just too terrified to hear them but we were moving. My horse was determined to catch up to the rest of them, with or without me. I held on for dear life as we clamored down the trail. Up until now I don't think I was ever so scared in my life. I had no idea how to control the horse beneath my now sore rear end, and he knew it! Without a filter or volume control, expletives spewed out of my mouth as I white-knuckled it through the woods. This was far from the hair blowing experience I thought I was going to have, and my knee throbbed with every gallop. The only time my horse stopped was to relieve himself—he even did *THAT* quickly! Once back on solid ground, I stayed far, far away from horses for probably close to 20 years!

An opportunity for a service exchange popped up. I would do Reiki on a friend's rescued horse in exchange for photography of the session. I expressed my fear of horses, then agreed despite my apprehension. As I drove to the stable I felt a slight comfort in the knowledge I would be near the horse and not *on* him!

The horse was tied up, and I approached cautiously with outstretched arms. At the onset I was incredibly mindful of how and where he was tied up, as well as my surroundings and "exit plan." The start of the session had me more in my "head" than in my heart. As the energy flowed through me to the horse, I relaxed and felt more and more comfortable in his presence. Inaudible fears were exchanged between us. He received what he needed from me, and my fear of horses began to shift. By the end of the session we leaned into each other in a way too powerful for words—our hearts understood. The experience left me with a longing to learn and to work with other horses. And so it was.

I learned from random horses in fields, rescued horses in zoos, client horses, and carriage pulling horses. Eventually, I tried horseback riding again, too. I rode locally a few times and gained enough confidence to try a longer ride in South Africa along Jeffreys Bay.

My traveling companion and I were part of a group of about a dozen riders. Two guides were up front, and I was second to last. The guy behind me was a self-proclaimed "expert rider." HA! We left the stable and rode through an open field toward Jeffreys Bay. There was a fairly steep dune that we needed to summit prior to arriving at the water. We approached slowly in single file. When the horse in front of me was near the top, my horse and I started our ascent. As we approached the top, I could hear Mr. Expert

Rider behind me.

"Uh oh, what the—? OH NO!" he said.

I turned and watched in slow motion as he and his saddle slid to the left. Mr. Expert Rider eventually hit the sand with a thud. His horse turned to the guy and grinned. I clearly heard the horse say, "I'll show you, expert rider."

What did I do? I yelled, "Man down! Man down!" as I encouraged my horse to continue up to level ground. I sent Reiki to my horse and the two other horses that figured out what I was doing while the guides helped Mr. Expert Rider back on his horse. The horses and I laughed and smiled the rest of the ride. I realized I was now part of the horse kingdom's "in crowd." (New horse clients who appeared after this trip included Louey and Diva.)

Fast-forward several years. I accepted an invitation to tent camp with wild horses on Assateague Island in Maryland. I wondered how different wild horses would be from the other horses I had met and worked with thus far in my lifetime. I also silently wondered if my 56-year-old body could still handle sleeping on the ground for three nights.

The approach to Assateague looked like the biggest hill of a roller coaster. I saw the incline but could not see what was on the other side of the peak until I was up there. It was beautiful! There was water on both sides as far as you could see. Once I was over the hump I saw five greeters: five beautiful horses grazing contentedly on the side of the road. The friend I was meeting was only 10 minutes ahead of me, yet she hadn't seen the horses. I already felt special and accepted by them.

Since we arrived late in the afternoon and rain was forecasted, we moved quickly to set up our tents up and eat dinner before hunkering down for the night. We were on the ocean side of the campground. I set my tent up in front of a fairly large section of bushes to block some of the ocean wind. There was an obvious archway in the bush leading to some kind of critter's home so I made sure not to erect my tent too close. I wasn't sure who lived there but I knew, for sure, something did! Without tracks or scat, I couldn't be sure what.

Our first night was rough. It wasn't long before I realized my tent was on a slight slope—but it was too late to do anything about it that night. The rain pounded. The wind bent and twisted my tent into a multitude of different shapes—like an amoeba on the move. Mother Nature's fury was relentless. My furry neighbors' sounds were familiar and close!

Crap! I thought to myself. *Raccoon—that's definitely a big raccoon.*

In my mind's eye, I could picture its hands. In my delirium, in the state between awake and sleep, I imagined its arms feeling around blindly and slipping under the tent's rainfly as it reached for the tent's zipper. My friend, in her tent some 30 or 40 feet away, couldn't possibly hear me ask, "Whose idea was this anyway?" over the pounding rain and howling wind. "My dad was a mailman." I kept telling myself. "Weather is in my genes. You're safe and dry—for now."

I took advantage of a short break in the weather and walked to the bathroom about a quarter of a mile away. The last thing I needed was a full bladder. I surely wasn't taking any chances peeing behind *my* tent in front of an unhappy raccoon! I settled back in my tent and tried to fall asleep. The next thing I heard was a stampede. A group of horses ran through our site. Oh, how I hoped they could see my tent. They were so close! I could feel the galloping vibration through my sleeping pad. The hard ground was definitely the least of my worries that first night, and sleep was nonexistent.

The next two days were filled with sunshine, laughs, exploring, and wildlife. We saw so many incredibly cool things. The island swarmed with wonder. Besides the wild horses and Rocky (or Rachel) Raccoon, there were bald eagles, a blue heron, an egret, a green heron, a turtle, the largest and greenest grasshoppers I'd ever seen, and a praying mantis. On one of our treks I spotted something bright green that hung from a distant tree. The color was so vivid it looked manufactured. As we got closer I could see it blowing in the wind. It was a snake! The bottom half of its body was coiled around a tree branch and the top half dangled and happily swung in the breeze. As we drove out of that area of the park, a long black rat snake scooted across the roadway right in front of our car! We stopped and watched in amazement at how fast it moved. In that moment I even felt its fear—fear of getting run over!

On our last day I decided to shower at the group campground. The showers were larger, had hooks for clothes, and a long bench where you could spread out your toiletries. As far as cold water showers go, they were like The Ritz. They were also deserted—not a soul of any kind in sight. As a result I decided to leave my phone AND my camera in the car.

I was very happy with myself and the decision to shower away from the other campers. It was quiet with plenty of room to spread out my stuff and keep it dry while I showered. A hot shower would have been nicer, but I made the best of it. I hummed and whistled as I began to undress. *This has been an amazing trip,* I thought to myself. *A short, spontaneous getaway to a new place was just what my soul had been craving.*

There's a system to taking a cold water shower when the air temperature is barely 70 degrees. I leaned forward to get only my head wet. "Brrrr that's cold," I told myself as the rest of my body shuddered. Still smiling, I applied shampoo, lathered, and rinsed—careful not to get the rest of me wet just yet. Outside, I heard what sounded like kids running by—and laughing. *Oh well,* I thought. *My privacy and quiet time was short-lived.*

I prepared for the next steps: wet and wash the arms, legs, and feet. "Uh oh" audibly spilled out of my mouth as I glanced over at the huge gap between the bottom of the shower door and the floor. Legs. There was a pair of horse legs just outside of my shower door. My excited childlike giggle immediately morphed into a gasp when I realized where my phone and camera were. The huge, awesome shower I was in appeared more like a jail cell now. It had white cinderblock walls, a sink/shower combo, small windows up really high and terrible lighting. *Crap. Now what?* I thought to myself.

Hot water. I definitely got myself into some hot water. At a minimum I had to finish my shower and dress. I prepared for the hardest part of the shower—the core and privates. Once the water button is pushed, it takes a few seconds for the water to actually come out. I pressed it and braced myself for the icy water to hit the most sensitive parts of my body. I lathered and rinsed and spun in circles while doing a crazy tiptoe dance in an effort to try and convince my body it was having fun. I'm fairly certain the Native American Indian spirits and the wild horses were amused by the sounds that were coming out of my cell, I mean, shower stall.

"Done," I said as I reached for my towel. The legs were gone! I hurriedly dried and dressed and gathered my stuff and headed for freedom, uh, for the door.

"Oh please, oh please," I said as I turned the knob and pushed open the door ever so slightly—and slowly. I peeked out. The coast was clear in front of me but I couldn't see what was behind the door OR around the corner of the building in the direction of my car. I looked to the right—around the edge of the door. I was within striking distance from the business end of one of the wild horses. Fortunately, he was busy drinking water from a leaky faucet. As I turned my head in the opposite direction, three more wild horses turned the corner just feet from where I was standing. I retreated to my cell and closed the door.

I wondered what time it was and how long I had been gone. I wondered if my camping friend was wondering where I was, or if she would come looking for me. I wondered who would believe me without pictures. The legs moved away from the door so I opened it again.

There was a couple. They were biking and stopped to look at the horses and take pictures. I waved from my cell as if they were my long-lost visitors. They laughed. The horses circled my shower building. They laughed, too. I wasn't sure I'd ever get out.

I forgot who I was. In that moment I had given away all my power and forgot how to use my gifts. I reasoned the cold shower must have temporarily frozen my brain. I collected my thoughts, centered myself, and connected with my guides. I energetically connected to the horse blocking my path and looked right into his soul.

"Dude, you done having fun? Are you going to let me out now?"

With that, the horse immediately shook his head up and down in the affirmative and stepped out of my way. He followed with the sound all horses make when they're content.

I walked confidently to the car, knowing I have finally arrived and I know who I am. It has taken courage, patience, perseverance, persistence and, above all, a sense of humor. Whatever walk you walk I wish for you the same success. I promise you the bumps are worth it.

Chapter 24
Timmy, Tux, & Trust

Extremely shy children do well around goofy adults they can trust. Many years ago I happened to spend a lot of time with two extremely shy children. I was the trustworthy, goofy adult. The children had a huge black and white cat named Timmy that felt safest watching everyone from the top of the refrigerator. Not surprisingly, he also felt safe and calm in my arms. He was a handsome boy indeed!

I tried all kinds of things to get these shy kids to open up and talk or laugh or engage with me. I made up stories and talked nonsense about what we would eat or whose turn it was to choose what or where we would eat. I'd pretend to trip over something that wasn't there or pretend I couldn't find them. If I was lucky, I might catch a sheepish grin as they turned away to hide their amusement. They loved every minute of it and, truthfully, so did I. One day I hit the jackpot.

Their parents and paternal grandparents were big churchgoers. So naturally, the children went, too. I had spent enough time in the church environment to know a few songs and prayers. I knew a few words here and there and some melodies—enough to get me by. Enter the song, *Jesus Loves the Little Children,* Sherri style. While driving the duo to swimming lessons, I spontaneously broke out in song. "Timmmmeeeee loves the little chilllllldren...alllllll the children of the worrrrrrld." In my rearview mirror, I could see the two in the back seat look at each other and bop their heads slightly in recognition of the song. I continued, "Purple, pink, and polka dot—even kids that cry a lot—Timmmmmmeeee loves the little children of the world!

I could see their expressions of confusion but they remained quiet and didn't say a word. Amused myself, I repeated the song, this time a little louder. Nothing! I sang it a few more times, even louder all the way to our destination—still nothing. On the way back from the lessons I was asked to "sing that song." I asked, "What song?" In unison, with swinging feet and huge smiles, they responded, "THE TIMMY SONG!" I agreed to sing it under one condition—that they sung it with me—and sing they did!

Timmy lived long enough to meet the children's third sibling but crossed over the rainbow bridge not long after. I remember him fondly and can still feel the weight of his body in my arms when I think about him from time to time. I am sure he continues to watch over those children since I no longer can. I do miss Timmy, but not as much as I miss those three children.

Fast-forward several years. A free roaming black and white tuxedo cat occasionally showed up in my driveway for a meal. He was definitely as handsome as Timmy but much leaner and younger. His dirty white paws and crooked whiskers told me he was a street cat. He would come around to eat and leave. There wasn't a whole lot of pomp and circumstance. This cat was all business. Attempts to talk, play, and offer Reiki were fruitless. The neighbor up the street told me that this cat had a circuit. He'd take turns eating at the neighbor's house, my house, a house on the next block, and only god knows how many of the restaurant dumpsters that are also within walking distance. Sometimes I'd see him every day for days, and sometimes I wouldn't see him at all for weeks.

One winter day he showed up looking sick, sneezing, and wheezing. His eyes were crusty, and his nose was running. The cat, now affectionately called Tux by my neighbor and me, was clearly miserable. I got medicine and started putting it into his food. I also asked the neighbor *not* to feed him until Tux finished his cycle of antibiotics. His kitty cat cold cleared up nicely, and he returned to his regular circuit.

Several months later I noticed his fur was thinning. I sent a picture to a trusted vet who responded, "Fleas," and told me what to put into his food. I watched him walk up to the food with the one-time flea treatment and walk away. Baffled, I enlisted the help of another animal communicator to find out why. Without crusty eyes and a runny nose this time, he could smell the medicine and was afraid to eat it. He left the food at my house untouched as he checked his other sources. When my friend told him it was safe and would help get rid of the bugs, he told her, "I'll think about it, Maybe I'll go back later." When I looked the next morning, the food was gone. In no time Tux's fur filled back in and took on a wonderful shine. I later learned that the shine was probably from the sardines in oil he regularly shared with my neighbor.

The following fall I started having pain on my right side. Since I thought it was muscular, I kept putting off getting it checked. It would start to feel better, and then I'd tweak it. It would feel better, then not. This went on for months, and I ignored it.

Just before Christmas Tux showed up one day, and his fur looked wet in one spot on his right side. Something wasn't right but I couldn't get a good enough look to figure out the problem. The next day I got a really good look! He had a gash a few inches long in about the same spot I was having my pain. In that moment he and I had a little come to Jesus moment—and it would continue for the next few days as I worked out the logistics of what was to come.

"Dude," I said to him, "you did a really good job this time. I can't fix this on my own with medicine in your food. You're going to have to trust me."

"What about you?" he said. "If I go, you go."

"Okay, buddy, I'll go see my doctor if you let me help you."

I don't know if having a conversation in my driveway with a feral cat qualifies me as a crazy cat lady or not, but I really don't care. What I do know is that this cat negotiated a deal with me based on mutual trust. His behavior through the process of trapping, vetting, and after-care would tell me, for sure, if he was bluffing or not.

My animal communicator friend and I talked him through the process of what he could expect if he let me help him get patched up. We explained the trap, the trip to the shelter, the trip to the vet, what would be done at the vet, the return to the shelter, the return to my house, and possibly having to spend one or more nights in each of those locations, as well as possibly being in lockdown somewhere to ensure the postsurgical antibiotics got into his system. We also let him know that the choice was his. He could trust me to help him or he could choose to continue on with a gash in his side. We repeated this mantra until the day was chosen to trap him. Consequently, the day was also the same day I saw my primary physician for *my* side pain.

I baited the trap with a can of chicken and gravy cat food, covered it with a towel laced with cat nip, told my friend to tell Tux that "today's the day," and went out for a walk. When I returned, Tux was in the trap.

"Thank you for trusting me, little buddy. The next step is to put you in the car and drive you to the shelter," I told him.

I readied the back hatch of my car with a plastic sled, just in case he had a potty accident, and gently placed the trap in it before closing the hatch. Softly, I spoke to him every step of the way. In all my years of working with feral cats, Tux was the calmest of the calm—a perfect gentleman. It felt wonderful to be trusted so completely. Looking back, I can relate to Tux's behavior—with all the abuse I suffered as a youngster I, too, was conditioned to hold my emotions in, especially fear!

Tux went to the veterinarian the morning after being trapped and was returned to the shelter later the same day. He was examined, neutered, ear tipped, wormed, stitched up, vaccinated, and started on antibiotics. I set up a place in my basement where his carrier could be inside an extra-large dog crate.

His carrier was in the back left corner of the crate and a litter box to the right. In front of his carrier was a fluffy blanket and, to the right of that, his food and water. Feral cats like the carrier in the crate arrangement because they have a place to retreat to when someone is cleaning the litterbox or refreshing the food. This arrangement would keep us both safe while he got his antibiotics. We would take things day by day.

I did my best to interact with him while still respecting his comfort level. During the day I would visit with him as frequently as he and my schedule would allow. Antibiotics were hidden in his breakfast and dinner, and he was surprised with treats at other times of the day. I would sit with him and read, talk to him, work on the computer, or play my steel tongue drum. Some days I would also try engaging him in play with a toy tied to the end of a string on a stick. Tux was definitely more interactive with me in the beginning, likely because of his pain meds. As the days went on, I felt he was missing the outside and his route. I did bring him outside (in his carrier) to get some fresh air but to him, it wasn't the same. Soon he would be finished with his antibiotics. I was torn.

Through the entire process I gave Tux options. He had the option to be helped or not, and he had the option of whether to become an indoor cat or not. As the pill count dwindled, my anxiety rose. He more than tolerated me, but I wouldn't call him

friendly and engaging. The whiskers that stood out straight when he was jacked up on pain meds were now curved down like a frown. It didn't take an animal communicator to figure out he was sad.

As I settled down to sleep the night before Tux's last dose of medicine, I asked the angels for guidance on how to proceed with Tux. That night I dreamt I came face to face with a tiger and he attacked my left hand. I couldn't have asked for a clearer sign than that!

I lovingly prepared Tux's breakfast with tears in my eyes. I crushed his last pill into dust and mixed it into a half of a can of wet Friskies chicken shreds. He especially loved the gravy. I dried my eyes and went down to the basement to feed him. He went into the carrier, and I closed it with a paint stick, like I had done every time before. I reached in, cleaned his litterbox, refreshed his water, and put the food in. I opened the carrier and closed and locked the crate. As soon as Tux felt safe again, he emerged to eat. When his food and medicine were gone, I told him, "A deal's a deal. You're free to leave." I put the rest of the can of food on the outside of his now opened crate.

Slowly and cautiously he looked around. His body was low to the ground as he carefully exited the crate. Once free, he ate from the can I placed just outside of it. I gave him a wide berth so he could either explore the rest of the basement or make a break for the outside. I told him I wished he would stay but reassured him the choice was his. Once he was done eating, he walked around the open door of the crate, tilted his head up toward the open stairway, and sniffed his way to the outside. He ate and left as he had countless times before. This time was different; this time it hurt. This time it ripped open an old wound I thought was healed.

I locked up the house and went for a walk on the towpath—I headed straight for Charlie's Stretch. The emotions I experienced were so raw. I sobbed as tears and snot ran down my face. The crazy notion that I would never ever see Tux again triggered me too deeply for words. I was inconsolable for most of the walk. Finally, one of my friends pointed out that he'd be back—that he wasn't dead or gone forever. "Just wait and see. You have to trust."

I found myself searching his favorite spots, frantically hoping to catch the smallest glimpse of him. I remembered similar feelings when those three young children were used as chess pieces in a game of adult drama and pulled from my life. I remembered how I hoped and prayed to accidentally bump into them sometime, somewhere. How I longed to see them or hear their laughter or voices. Tux leaving caused much of those emotions to resurface for healing and understanding.

Driving home from that walk, I saw a flash of something between parked cars on Main Street. It was a bad-ass black and white tuxedo cat with a patch of fur missing. In that bare spot the cat was sporting seven purple stitches. He was smiling and strutting like I'd never seen before. I could hear him telling everybody: "I'm back."

Tux has been back to my house and the neighbor's just about every day since. He's even come down into my basement on his own and looked around. He knows he is free to choose and knows I'm someone he can trust. Timmy's three children may still be caged in their parent's dysfunction but, in time, I trust they, too, will come back around to see me. I am patient, and I trust.

Chapter 25
The Truth

Imagine growing up with an underlying nagging feeling that something isn't quite right. I had others tell me how much my sibling loved me but it never felt authentic—it always felt staged. It felt as though these other family members were trying to convince *themselves* of something that simply wasn't true. It was much easier to deal with their fantasy than to make waves or take corrective action. It let them off the hook.

The truth is that many people saw the tension between my sibling and me. They saw it for years. It was the big pink elephant in the room, and NOBODY wanted to address it. I was always the adorable, loving, helpful, outgoing one—and my sibling was the quiet one I needed to "watch out for."

As a kid, I didn't know what I didn't know. I didn't know that such evil could be present in the same blood line. I accepted my sibling as my sibling, and accepted all the evil things that were done to me: the torture, manipulation, abuse, incessant name calling, and mockery. I accepted all of it and believed that I *was* those awful things I was called. I had no idea how those seeds would affect so many other parts of my life as an adult and how much work I would have to do to make myself whole again. These things were buried deep inside me for over 50 years—until I was deeply triggered, and the truth about my sibling surfaced.

In the earliest memory I was a toddler and shared a room with my sibling. Soon after "lights out" my sibling begged me to climb out of my crib and come to their bed. I was held tightly in a bear hold as my sibling yelled to our mother, "MA! Sherri's in my bed!" My mother returned me to my crib with a scolding. The scene played out multiple times each night as I trusted my sibling's repeated promises not to yell for our mother as her scolding escalated to beatings. Eventually, I would cry myself to sleep while my sibling laughed.

During a later memory I was eleven years old. I was fed alcohol during a New Year's Eve party by my sibling and their spouse to the point that I became falling down drunk. There were other "adults" present, including one of my cousins. All were at least eighteen years old. While all this was going on, my sibling's five-month-old baby slept in the next room. The scene didn't end there. They proceeded to strip me naked, throw me into the bathtub, and force me to drink black coffee—all while they laughed and took pictures.

They laughed again the next morning while telling me how I foamed at the mouth once I passed out. They laughed for days without any concern over how much worse that night could have been. Their actions could have ended my life.

Anyone who has grown up with a sibling like mine knows there were many more incidents between the two I described, and many more that followed that New Year's Eve. Yes, there is a normal amount of teasing that occurs between siblings growing up. What I experienced was far from normal and a disgusting abuse of power considering the seven-year age difference. Imagine paging through the ages: What chance does a two-year-old have against a nine-year-old, an eleven-year-old against an eighteen-year-old?

Forty some years later when I told the story to that "sleeping baby," I was met with a cold truth. The apple doesn't fall far from the tree. That baby's response as an adult? "How does *this* help us as a family?" There was no empathy, compassion, or understanding for what I went through as an eleven-year-old girl at the hands of that adult baby's parents. The truth is, if they wanted me to talk better about them, they should have treated me better. We are now almost five years out from the abuse surfacing. There has been ample opportunity for apologies and explanations and restitution, yet there has been only silence.

I survived the initial abuse, the resurfacing of the abuse, and my "family's" attempts at making it vanish by dismissing me and trying to minimize all of it. The truth is that I am finally free. I no longer have to shrink or hide for fear of upsetting a jealous sibling or their offspring. I know where my trust issues stem from, and now have the power, tools, and confidence to stop other would-be abusers in their tracks. I chuckle, knowing that I feel incredibly safer with wild or so-called unpredictable animals than I did around my blood family.

As I spoke openly about the abuse, I was met with disbelief on many sides. Few could look me in the eye and see the lifelong pain, hardship, and challenges it caused. It was easier to dismiss and further isolate me than to *listen* with an open heart. Some listened only enough to respond, rather than to understand how awful and terrifying a good part of my childhood was.

During my healing I mourned the loss of my entire living family. For a while I became that unloved, undusted piece of furniture in the corner again. And then, like a phoenix from the ashes, I resurfaced—stronger and more determined than ever.

I stopped crying about what I don't have and started seeing and celebrating what I *do* have. I have a heart, soul, and conscience, despite growing up in an incredibly unhealthy environment. I *finally* have ready access to people and tools that assist me in healing the multiple abuses (of power), trauma, and betrayal I endured. By escaping the chains of my family's dysfunction, I have a clear path. I have come to accept that the magical and loving animal bond I have runs far deeper than anything I thought I had with my bloodline.

I have a tribe of trusted friends and clients that I am incredibly grateful for. They have proven that their only motive is to love me and remind me who I am and the gifts I possess. They see me. They hear me. They love me. They remind me that I am an animal communicator, connected to Mother Earth with the heart and soul of a spiritual warrior who can weather any storm.

I have the same wish for you. Face your fears, uncover your gifts, and fuel your passions to heal your soul. Believe in yourself, believe you are worthy, and believe you deserve the best. The path isn't easy, but the results are certainly worth it! I believe in you. I also believe your truth shall set you free.

Live in love not in fear
—and that, my friend, is the truth.

I Am

I am a protector, because I was not protected.
I am loving, because I was not loved.
I am direct, because I lived in confusion.
I am vocal, because I was silenced.
I am fearless, because I lived in fear.
I am compassionate, because you were cruel.
I am empathetic, because you were apathetic.
I am trustworthy, because I kept your secrets.
I am supportive, because I was not supported.
I am understanding, because I was not understood.
I am vigilant, because I never saw it coming.
I am intuitive, to stay ahead of you.
I am independent, because you abused the system.
I work for what I want, because you manipulate others to get
what you want.
I am a warrior, because of your torture, torment, and taunting.
I am the black sheep, because you played your role so well.
I am resilient, because you will not defeat me.
I am so many things, because of you, in spite of you.
I am a survivor, because I was a victim.

Sherri A. Lynn, 2018

Resources

Through the years I've tried several different modalities to assist with my personal healing journey. The severe trauma and abuse I suffered affected me physically, emotionally, mentally, and spiritually. In addition to traditional "talk" therapy, I've tried (and recommend) everything listed below:

Emotional Freedom Technique (also known as EFT or tapping) – assists with pain and "moving" emotions through the body.

Eye Movement Desensitization and Reprocessing (also known as EMDR) – great for PTSD and clearing old thought patterns.

Family Constellation Therapy – assists with uncovering destructive family dynamics that may be hidden under the surface. It reveals entanglements that can lead to healing.

Past Life Regression – helps uncover past trauma and grief.

Meditation – relieves stress and anxiety, which leads to a greater sense of well-being.

Yoga – decreases stress and anxiety and offers many other health benefits.

Sound Therapy – releases energetic blockages that induce ease and harmony in the body.

Reiki – An ancient Japanese Energy Healing modality that works on all levels of a person's energy field.

IET® (Integrated Energy Therapy®) – a safe and gentle method for releasing energy blockages in the body.

Massage – manipulating soft tissues to release stress and tension and increase blood flow.

Bowen – uses gentle rolling hand movements to stretch the fascia and reduce the pain response.

Crystals – there are crystals to assist with all kinds of physical, mental, and emotional challenges; they are to be treated as sacred healing tools for best results.

Essential Oils – each oil or blend has a specific purpose; some promote relaxation while others may help with clarity or focus.

Each one helps to raise your vibration to promote a sense of well-being.

Flower Essences – similar to essential oils only they can be taken internally.

Sacred Women's Retreats – when properly run, retreats create a safe space for women to share and feel heard, appreciated, and supported.

Sweat Lodges – a sacred, spiritual group practice that helps promote deep healing and releasing on a soul level.

Jin Shin Juytsu – an ancient self-healing practice that promotes balance and well-being by holding different points on the body known as safety energy locks.

Forest Bathing – immersing yourself in nature in a mindful way to reconnect to who you really are.

Intermittent Fasting – Healthy Body, Health Mind

Sacred travel to places known for energy vortexes and healing energies – Sedona, Machu Picchu, India, South Africa, Utah canyons, The Smokey Mountains, The White Mountains, The Adirondacks, The Rockies, Hawaii.

Recommended Reading

Sibling Abuse by Vernon R. Weihe
Homecoming: Reclaiming and Championing Your Inner Child by John Bradshaw
The Body Keeps the Score by Bessel Van Der Kolk
Getting Past Your Past by Francine Shapiro
A Girl Raised by Wolves by Lockey Maisonneuve
The Courage to Change – One Day at a Time in Al-Anon II
Adult Children of Alcoholics – Adult/Dysfunctional Families
Braving the Wilderness by Brené Brown
Daring Greatly by Brené Brown

Acknowledgments

My heart is so full of gratitude for my writers group—Karen, Wendy, and Jack started as strangers yet managed to create a safe place for me to tell my stories and grow as a writer. Without their loving support, guidance, and encouragement, this book would not have come to be.

Thank you, Wendy, Sam, Mike, and the rest of the IET® (Integrated Energy Therapy®) angels for keeping my energy clear during this process. Knowing you were all there kept me on track. I'm sending continued love and abundance to all of you.

Much love to my soul family—the friends, clients, pets (here and gone), and soul sisters who took part and encouraged me along the way. Whether your animal made it into this book or not, they were still an integral part of my growth, development, and healing. If you were by my side as I worked or you heard about any of the stories before this book was printed, you helped—and I thank you! You know who you are!

Thank you, Open Door Publications, Eric Labacz Design & Illustration, and Greg Backman Photography for all the work you've done to put this book together. It has been an honor and a pleasure to have you in my circle. I wish continued peace and success to you all.

About the Author

Photo by Greg Backman

Sherri has learned that it's hard to hit a moving target. As such, she keeps herself active hiking, biking, playing softball, kayaking, camping, and whatever else calls to her sense of adventure in the moment. She's likely to be found playing outside—anywhere there may be animals, or well-behaved children in any kind of weather. With more lives than a cat and similar to the Phoenix, Sherri has reinvented herself a number of times during her existence. Through it all one thing remains constant: her love for animals, nature, and spirit. Sherri currently makes her home in New Jersey with Chase, Spooky, and Tux (the neighborhood feral) calling all the shots.

Sherri's work experience is as diverse as a mutt's DNA. She is a retired Information Technology professional and former elected official who now spends her "spare time" as a Minister officiating weddings, a Reiki Master, an Integrated Energy Therapy® Master Instructor, a Rutgers Pet Care School Presenter, a County Animal Response Team leader, a Lehigh River Rafting Guide and only God knows what else she'll add to the list before this book goes to print. People often ask her, "Is there anything you can't do?" The answer is always the same: "I can't cut straight with scissors."

She hopes to someday perform standup comedy and live off the grid on an animal sanctuary with like-minded individuals. You can learn more about her at www.reikipaws.com, on her Facebook page at https://tinyurl.com/ysf823us, or on LinkedIn at https://www.linkedin.com/in/sherri-lynn-4b5b3911/.

If you enjoyed this book, please leave a review at Amazon.com today.

Made in the USA
Middletown, DE
21 May 2021